D0029097

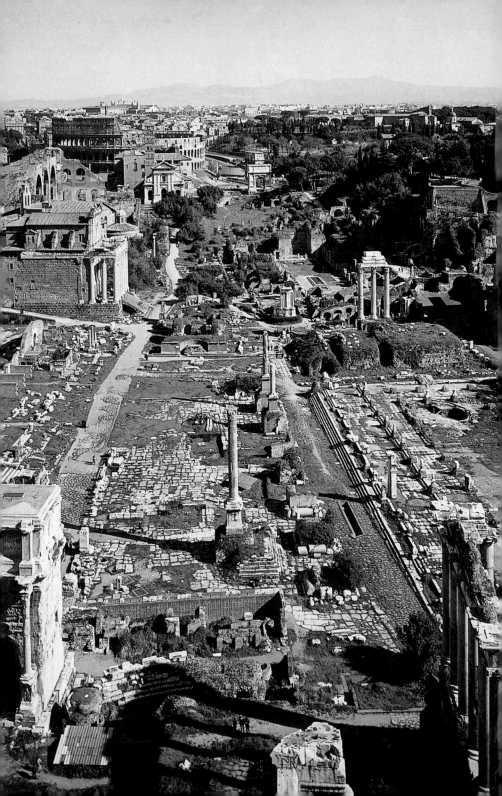

ANCIENT

ROME

Art, architecture and history

Ada Gabucci

Edited by Stefano Peccatori
and Stefano Zuffi

Translated by T. M. Hartmann

THE J. PAUL GETTY MUSEUM
LOS ANGELES

Contents

Browsing Guide

In order to offer the reader a useful tool for information and study that is easy and fun to browse through, this volume is divided into three subsections. These are recognizable by colored tabs: yellow is for the pages dedicated to art and architecture, blue denotes those parts concerned with historical and artistic background, and pink refers to an analysis of specific masterpieces of art. Every pair of pages goes into depth on a given subject with an introduction and commentary on illustrations and photos. The reader can freely choose how and in what order to browse through this book, by either leafing through the chapters in order or developing a more personal approach.

Maps and indexes of places and names complete the information provided in this book. These too are illustrated in order to allow for immediate identification of various works, historical figures, and geographic locations.

■ On page 2: The Roman Forum was built in a marshy area that had previously been used as a burial site.

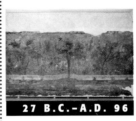

27 B.C.–A.D. 96

The Empire's Beginnings and Establishment

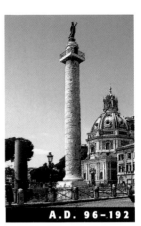

A.D. 96–192

The Height of the Empire: From Trajan to the Antonines

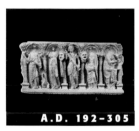

A.D. 192–305

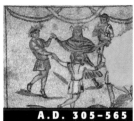

A.D. 305–565

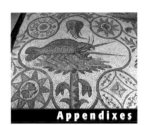

Appendixes

Crisis in the Empire: From the Severans to the Tetrarchy

The Fall of the Empire: Epilogue to an Ancient World

The Roman Republic Begins to Assert Itself

According to tradition, Rome was founded on April 21, 753 B.C. The early centuries are difficult to reconstruct, and distinguishing legend from history is extremely complex. Archeological data does sustain, however, that the Etruscans were already dominant between the seventh and sixth centuries B.C., and this lends support to the legend that the fifth and seventh kings were the founders of Tarquinia. Rome was already a blossoming city by the end of the sixth century B.C., and thanks to its strategic location, the city became a necessary stop on many commercial routes. The first monuments and public works, such as the Cloaca Maxima (The Great Drain), began to spring up in the city's center at that time. The Roman Republic began in 509 B.C. when the city government passed into the hands of consuls, pairs of magistrates that were elected annually. By the fourth century B.C. Rome had become an expanding power, opening diplomatic relations through treaties and alliances. After a series of wars with neighboring territories and various attempts to overcome diverse social problems, the republic was soon in control of all the peoples of central Italy and Magna Graecia. In the third century B.C., and with the Punic Wars, Rome began to focus its interest on the Mediterranean.

▼ A hut-shaped urn from the Iron Age found in the burial grounds of the Roman Forum. Forty-one tombs have been found in the archaic cemetery that probably once took up most of the valley. The most recent tombs date from the beginning of the eighth century B.C.

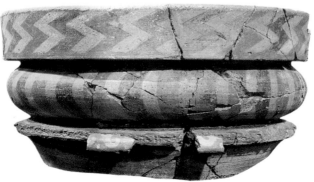

◄ Multicolored clay façade from the end of the fourth century B.C. This clay fragment was discovered during excavations near the Temple of Magna Mater and has been interpreted as either a capital or a facing for a base of a wooden column. Rome, Palatine Museum.

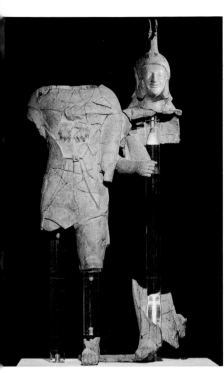

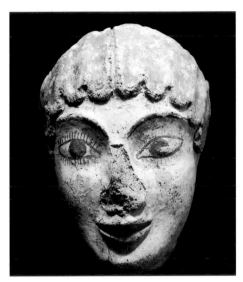

◀ Hercules and Athena, from the middle of the sixth century B.C. This group of clay statues was arranged in the area of Sant'Omobono, near the temples of Luck and Mater Matuta. According to tradition these two were created by Servius Tullius and date to 579–534 B.C.

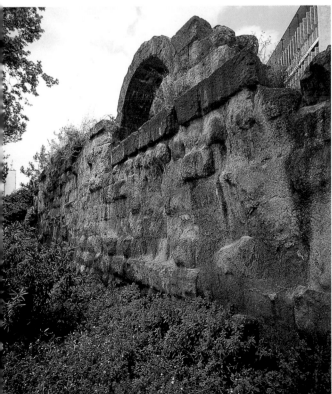

▲ A feminine antefix of painted clay dating from the end of the sixth century B.C. This small head was probably made by a Latin artisan and shows small traces of Greek and Etruscan influences. It was one of the vertical decorations along the eaves of a roof. Rome, Palatine Museum.

◀ An arch from the Severan walls in Rome. The arch was built on the Aventine hill in the first century B.C. It is situated in part of a wall tradition- ally attributed to Servius Tullius and was built to accommodate catapults. After the Gauls of Brenno sacked Rome in 387 B.C., another set of walls was built of tufa rock from Grotta Oscura.

Toward an Empire

▶ The Hall of Isis on Palatine hill, circa 25 B.C. The hall had a rectangular shape with an apse and was discovered under the basilica of the Flavian imperial residence. It owes its name to the presence of devotional symbols to Isis on the walls and the vault that were designed in the "second style" (see page 36).

After destroying Carthage, Rome began to concern itself with preventing any future threats to its interests and continued extending its territory. This new perspective necessarily brought with it an impending clash with the Hellenistic kingdoms, who would keep the Romans busy throughout all of the second century B.C. In the end, between 149 and 146 B.C., Greece and Macedonia became Roman provinces, and Carthage was definitively crushed. By century's end, Rome was already dominating a good part of the Mediterranean and counted eight provinces. Notable riches began to pour in, mostly into the hands of the nobles. Most of the population, however, had been ruined by the wars, having abandoned their farming. A period of dissent and internal strife followed, along with further wars of conquest. During this time, powerful figures emerged who progressively threatened the republican system. One of these was Marius, who was elected consul for six consecutive years. Another was Sulla, who took up arms and marched against Rome. Above all, there was Caesar. Having decided to install a monarchical regime, he perpetuated a dictatorship with all the trappings of Hellenistic and Eastern regality.

▼ Pompey. Commissioned by the emperor's descendants around A.D. 30, the statue is a copy of an original that portrayed him when he was in his fifties in 50 B.C. Copenhagen, Ny Carlsberg Glyptothek.

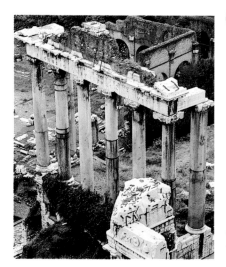

◀ The Temple of Saturn in Rome. The temple was first built in the fifth century B.C., but the ruins that dominate the entire southern corner of the Roman Forum were restructured beginning in A.D. 42 and restored after the fire of A.D. 283.

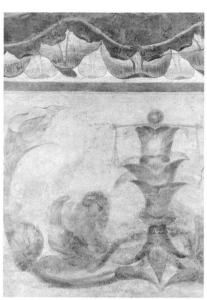

▼ Julius Caesar. This statue is a marble copy of an original work in bronze made during the last years of Caesar's life. Born in 100 B.C., he was assassinated on March 15, 44 B.C. and died at the foot of a statue of Pompey. In his will, Caesar left three hundred sesterces to every Roman citizen. Turin, Museo di Antichità.

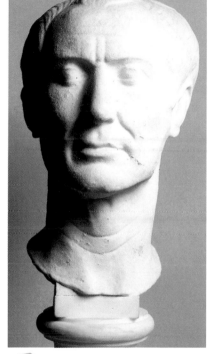

◄ A Galatian suicide. This marble statue and two companion pieces were copies of a bronze group commissioned by King Attalus the 1st of Pergamum at the end of the third century B.C. to celebrate his triumph over the Galatians. The marble copies, which Julius Caesar displayed to celebrate his victory over the Gauls, decorated the garden of his villa on Quirinal hill. Rome, Palazzo Altemps.

A wall painting of a garden created during the Augustan period in the Livia Villa in Prima Porta. Rome, Palazzo Massimo alle Terme.

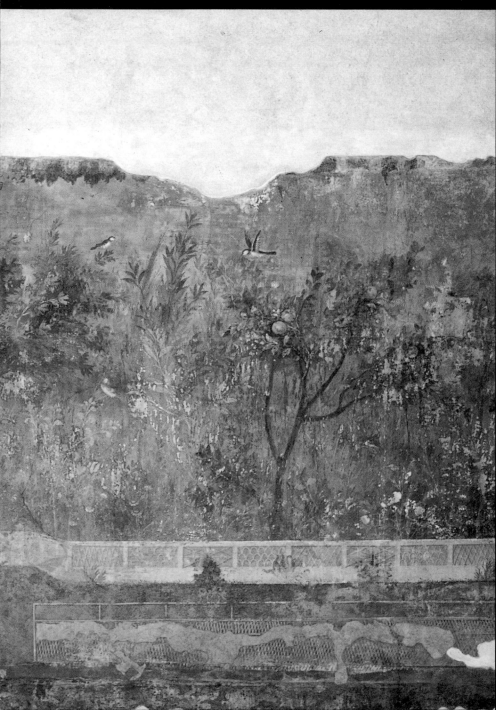

The Empire's Beginnings and Establishment

The *Pax Augusta:* Ideology and Propaganda

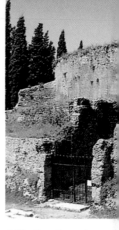

As Augustus himself narrates with pride in the history of his exploits, the *Res Gestae*, the Senate ordered the Temple of Janus closed three times during his long reign, something only permitted during peacetime. For the emperor's contemporaries, who had never seen those doors shut before, this gesture meant an end to a period of lengthy and bloody civil wars. Though the state was armed and ready to repress any attempt from within or without to destabilize the newly found order, the Augustan peace meant a return to civil life and a noteworthy economic boom. This well-being even reached the farthest provinces of the empire, and these areas were integrated into the social and economic life of the Roman world. Even the emperor reinvented himself. As Octavian, he was a virile, warring general who was a strict and decisive commander; as Augustus, he became a gracious celebrity, reluctant to receive honors and charges, except to please those who he himself had empowered to offer them to him. He became respectful of traditions, restored traditional morality and family values, and allowed imperial worship to develop around him.

▲ The Mausoleum of Augustus in Rome. This grandiose tomb was built in Campus Martius beginning in 29 B.C. and perhaps was modeled after Alexander the Great's sepulcher. The prince had seen the tomb in Alexandria, Egypt.

▶ This pendant, which glorifies Augustus, perhaps memorializes Tiberius's triumph over the Germans in A.D. 7. The prince is seated next to the goddess Roma and is being crowned by Oikoumene, the personification of universal power. Vienna, Kunsthistorisches Museum.

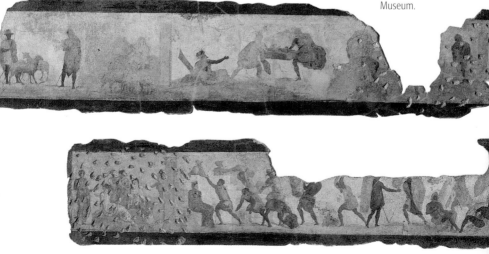

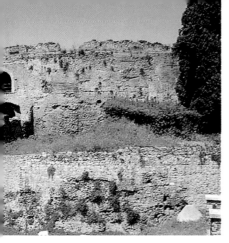

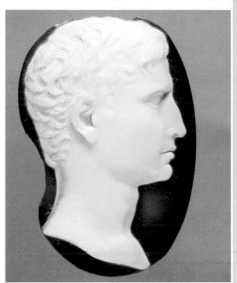

► A cameo of the young Augustus from Herculaneum. The fact that a portrait of the prince has been placed on a personal object recalls prevalent attitudes at the beginning of the new regime of flaunting loyalty.

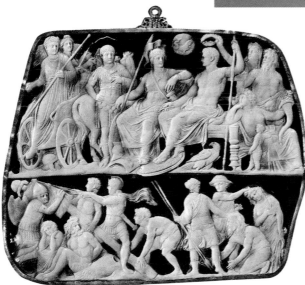

▼ A painted frieze from Esquiline hill dating to the early Augustan period. The frieze decorated the walls of a small columbarium, and in a series of episodes distributed among various pillars, it narrates the myth of Rome's origins. The story of Aeneas is on one side, while on the other Mars and Rhea Silvia meet and Romulus and Remus are born. In the central scene of the upper fragment, the twins are left on the banks of the Tiber, while the lower fragment shows the saga of Aeneas and Ascanius. Rome, Palazzo Massimo alle Terme.

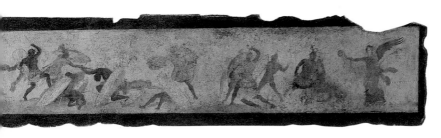

The Augustan Style

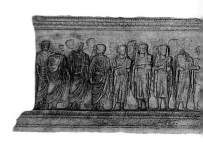

The refined, aristocratic, and impersonal art of the Augustan age was maintained with little variation for the entire Julio-Claudian dynasty. It represents a quest for perfection in technique and form and has been celebrated as a high point of Roman art. In reality, it was expression that was appropriated from the official and political world it served. Augustan art sought, just as the prince did, to build a link between the traditions of the Hellenistic kingdoms and the Roman Republic. Nonclassical elements, mostly from Italic and Hellenistic traits that remained in local artisan traditions, emerge only occasionally in the Augustan style. Neoatticism, a revival of Greek styles, was an artistic current in the first century B.C. that copied and was inspired by Greek works from the fifth and fourth centuries B.C. There was never really the chance for a new, autonomous artistic current to form. What results are works of cold elegance, a particular slant toward retrospective tastes, and an eclecticism that mixes general Italic concepts with diverse decorative solutions derived from the artistic trends of Hellenism.

▼ Marcellus, from the end of the first century B.C. This posthumous portrait of Augustus's son-in-law, who died in 23 B.C., is an example of Augustan classicism. The young man is portrayed as Hermes, and the statue is signed by "Cleomene of Athens, son of Cleomene." Paris, Louvre.

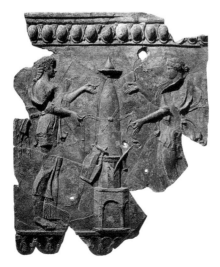

◄ A multicolored slab of terra cotta depicting two girls decorating a cone-shaped symbol for Apollo. The slab probably decorated an interior frieze of the Temple of Apollo on Palatine hill, along with numerous others that similarly featured two figures facing one another. Rome, Museo Palatino.

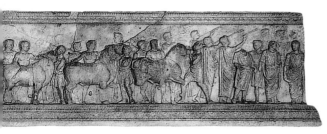

◀ A procession of street magistrates *(vicomagistri)* with priests, musicians, and animals for sacrifice. This base is from Palazzo della Cancelleria and dates to the first half of the first century A.D. Vatican City, The Vatican Museums.

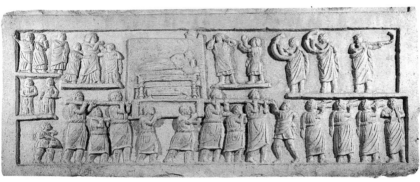

▲ A relief from Amiternum with a funeral procession from the second half of the first century B.C. The piece accurately describes the events of a funeral with the deceased, or a representation of the body, raised up on its side with a starry background. L'Aquila, Museo Nazionale d'Abruzzo.

▶ This clay head of Apollo dates from the end of the first century B.C. and is possibly from Augustus's first residence on Palatine hill or another area of the late republican period. The austere ideology of the prince seems underlined by the choice of such poor material as terra cotta for this piece. Rome, Palazzo Massimo alle Terme.

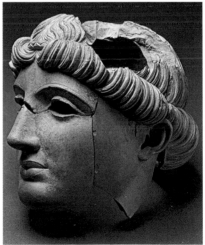

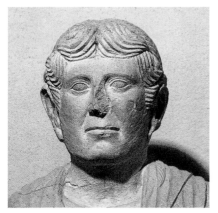

◀ A detail from a funerary statue of a woman, from the end of the first century B.C. The face is quite unique and is framed by hair that is combed according to the style of the time, as Octavian's sister Octavia and Antonia wore theirs.

In the arc of four centuries, hairstyle fashions for Roman women changed radically, beginning in the late republican period. Portraits of empresses and princesses that have survived help to date the different fashions. Aquileia, Museo Archeologico.

A Portrait of Augustus

The power of Augustus was not just defined by a single office he held, but rather a combined sum of charges and traditional honors attributed to him. Sometimes he appeared as consul, with a red-bordered toga; as a priest; or a victorious general, crowned and wearing a purple toga. Augustus was portrayed as commander in a bronze statue around the year 20 B.C. that was modeled after Polyclitus's *Doryphorus*, the prototype of all Roman statues of figures in breastplate armor. The prince, arm raised, asks for silence and is wearing a richly decorated cuirass with elaborate symbols that would eventually be developed for propaganda uses. The image has survived to this day through a marble copy that Augustus's wife Livia Drusilla requested for her villa at Prima Porta after the death of her husband. The pontifical statue of Augustus, on the other hand, where the prince is possibly attending a sacrifice, fully expresses piety (*pietas*), a filial attitude toward the Roman gods. A hem of the toga has been raised in order to cover his head. When Augustus assumed the position of head pontiff when Lepidus died in 12 B.C., piety was one of the virtues he made ample use of in his political program.

▼ The statue of Augustus at Prima Porta. The lorica statue, meaning with a cuirass or breastplate, is a marble copy of a bronze original from 20 B.C. Vatican City, The Vatican Museums.

◄ A statue of Livia from the end of the first century B.C., from the Tiber. This hairstyle, with a type of knot toward the front, was introduced as a conservative reaction to the complicated hairdos of the republican period. Rome, Palazzo Massimo alle Terme.

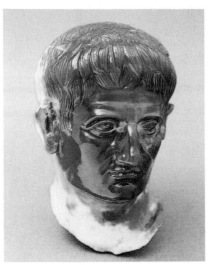

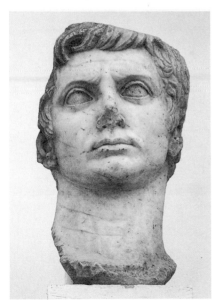

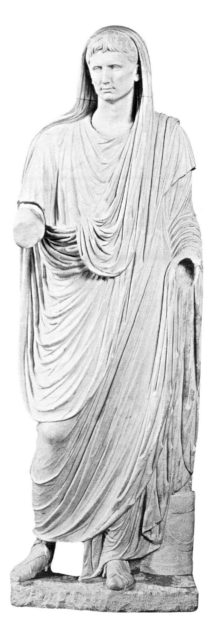

◄ Augustus, circa A.D. 98–103. This small head is made from Indian sardonyx and was actually once a statue of Domitian. The lines and hair were successfully reworked and modeled after the statue of Augustus at Prima Porta. Saragozza, Italy, Museo.

▲ Augustus, from Italica in present-day Spain. The colossal dimensions of this head—which is seventy-three centimeters high—and the facial expression help to date this piece to the age of Tiberius and Claudius. Seville, Museo Arquéologico Provincial.

► Augustus as pontiff, from the end of the first century B.C. or the beginning of the first century A.D., from Via Labicana in Rome. The head and forearm are made of Greek marble, while the rest is in Italic marble. Rome, Palazzo Massimo alle Terme.

The *Ara Pacis*

The *Ara Pacis*—the altar of peace—was made by Greek sculptors and is the key monument in understanding the politics, ideology, and art of the Augustan period. The enclosure that surrounds the altar is ornately decorated with friezes of leaves and depictions of people. Near the doorway four panels retell the myth of Rome's origins with allegorical scenes. A long procession along the side walls recalls the dedication of the altar on January 30, 9 B.C. The entire imperial family, down to the smallest of children, is scrupulously represented and recognizable.

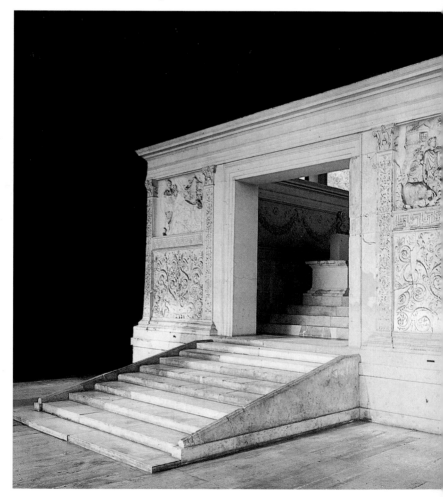

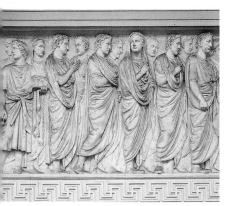

◀ A detail of the procession from a frieze on the north side. In this relief, all the heads of the priests had been lost but were possibly restored in the eighteenth century. The entire north-side frieze– the least important–is less preserved than the one on the south side.

▼ *Saturnia Tellus*, from a frieze on the east side. This is a complex allegory with a maternal figure seated with two children on her lap. She is seated between two semi-nude nymphs, whose cloaks are blown by the wind. One is seated on a sea dragon; the other, on a swan. The landscape in the background has also been carefully sculpted.

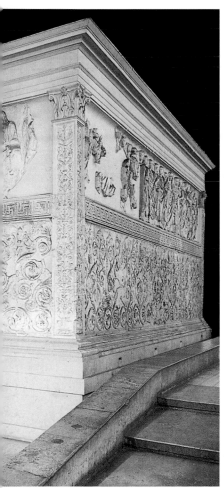

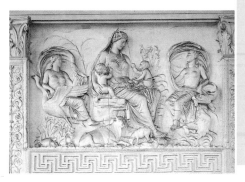

▼ The *Ara Pacis* is made up of a rectangular, marble enclosure built on a platform accessible by a stairway. At the center is a working altar. The external walls are entirely decorated by reliefs.

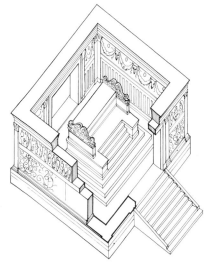

Artistic Craftwork

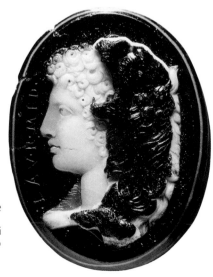

Crafts made from precious materials such as silver, amber, ivory, and other stones were intended for the upper classes, who did not usually care for things that were too innovative. Most favored works by Greek artists, and it was in imitating these that Augustan art reached its highest and most characteristic point in refined silver work, engraved gems, carved amber, and glass cameos. The artisans drew their inspiration for these works from treasures of the Hellenistic and Eastern courts such as Pergamum, Syria, and Alexandria. Their work was considered exemplary during the entire imperial period. Toreutics in particular—the art of creating embossed metal containers—blossomed and reached a technical high point during the Augustan age. This is not only witnessed by the discovery of important silver treasures but also by the imitation of metal vases with stamped clay, glazed ceramic, and glass work. Besides toreutics, engraving was also in fashion during this period, and despite its cold tone, techniques were often quite refined.

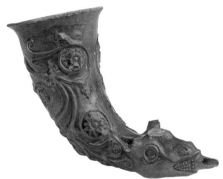

▲ A glazed ceramic horn with an antelope's head from the Augustan period. The decorative foliage points to the possible work of a Venetian workshop. Turin, Museo di Antichità.

▶ A cameo of Hercules in a lion headdress from the Augustan period. Created by a sculptor from Alexandria, this piece is made of three layers of sardonyx. From the Medici collections, Naples, Museo Archeologico Nazionale.

ART AND ARCHITECTURE

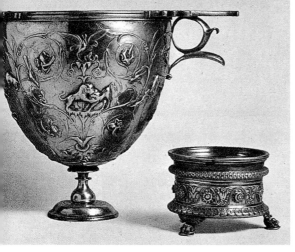

◄ A vase and salt holders from the first century A.D. These objects were part of a treasure trove of almost thirty kilograms of silver, mostly tableware and toiletry objects. They were discovered in a Roman villa with wall paintings in the small Vesuvian town of Boscoreale that was destroyed by the eruption of Mount Vesuvius in A.D. 79. The vase's ornamentation is especially refined with vines, animals, and hunting scenes. Paris, Louvre.

► This vase, made from transparent quartz originally from Egypt, was found in Santa Maria Capua Vetere. It dates to the Augustan period, as can be seen from its shape and leafy designs. Naples, Museo Archeologico Nazionale.

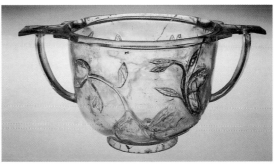

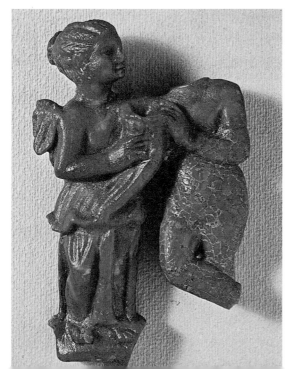

◄ Eros and Psyche, from an amber group of funeral decorations from the middle of the first century A.D. Amber, a precious, fossilized resin, was carried in rough pieces by glaciers from the Baltic Sea. It crossed the alpine paths to Aquileia, where able artisans carved it and created prized items that were quite costly. In the middle of the first century A.D., Pliny lamented, "one figurine, no matter how small, costs more than healthy, living men." Aquileia, Museo Archeologico Nazionale.

27 B.C.–A.D. 96

Livia's Villa

A painted garden of plants, trees, and birds adorns the walls of an underground hall without windows. Part of Livia's villa, located on Via Flaminia at Prima Porta, it was perhaps a room for resting in summer. Rome, Palazzo Massimo alle Terme.

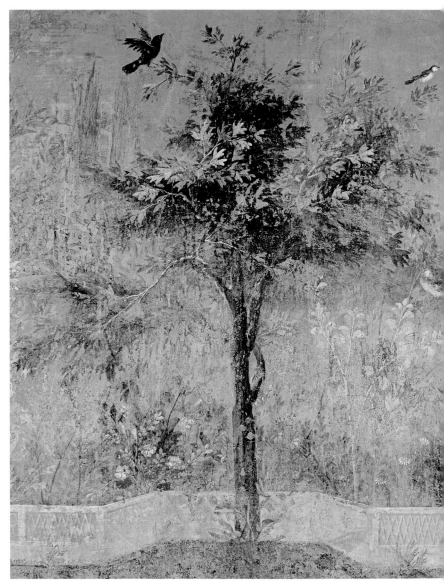

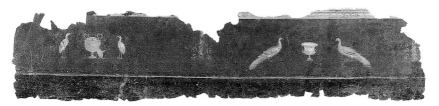

▲ A fresco in the third style (see page 36) dating from the end of the first century B.C. It was once near the river port of San Paolo a Roma. Pairs of birds facing each other with a vase between each of them have been designed with precision in miniature on the red background of the baseboard. Rome, Palazzo Massimo alle Terme.

▶ From the Farnesina villa, triclinium C, on the left wall. The complex decorative scheme of the villa seems centered around motifs that are linked to Augustan propaganda. It was probably built when Julia, daughter of Augustus, and Agrippa were married in 19 B.C. Rome, Palazzo Massimo alle Terme.

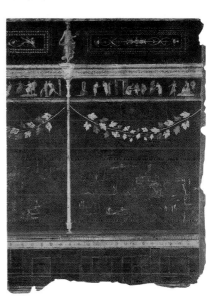

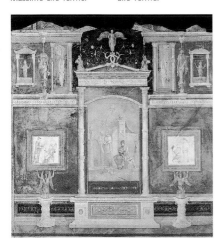

▲ From the Farnesina villa, cubicle B, on a wall at the end of an alcove. In the center niche is Dionysos as a child between the nymphs of Nissa, while the sides feature invented architecture and pavilions with similar scenes. Rome, Palazzo Massimo alle Terme.

▶ Panels of a floor mosaic from the first century B.C. from the threshold of a triclinium of a Roman villa near a group of houses of San Basilio on Via Nomentana. The multicolored effect was achieved with differently shaped, colored tiles with a variety of patterns in the mosaic. Rome, Palazzo Massimo alle Terme.

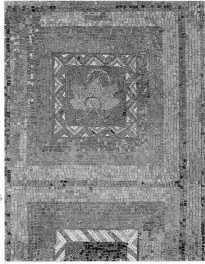

The Provinces: Narbonesis Gaul

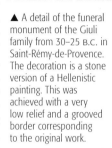

The western provinces of the empire developed significantly during the Augustan age, thanks in part to a restructuring of how the provinces were governed and a settling of the situation of war veterans. During this time, certain fundamental characteristics of provincial art started, based on the plebeian artistic tradition already in use by the middle class. This tradition became a founding current in the colonies together with graphic and iconographic traits of official Augustan art. Narbonesis Gaul played an important role. Today there are reliefs, arches, and funerary monuments decorated in a rich, picturesque style in Saint-Rémy-de-Provence, Carpentras, and Orange that have free-space solutions far superior to any of their contemporaries in Rome. This artistic current was confirmed by excavations dating to Hellenistic times at Glanum (Saint-Rémy) containing sculptures like those at Pergamum. These discoveries were surely linked to the Greek origins of remote outposts found on the Gallic coast and immediately inland. The monument that most symbolizes the conquest of the Alps is the Trophaeum Alpium. Built by Augustus in 7 or 6 B.C. at the border between Italy and the Maritimae Alpes, it could be seen by navigators and wayfarers traveling from Italy to Gaul or Spain.

▲ A detail of the funeral monument of the Giuli family from 30–25 B.C. in Saint-Rémy-de-Provence. The decoration is a stone version of a Hellenistic painting. This was achieved with a very low relief and a grooved border corresponding to the original work.

▼ Pont du Gard, from the end of the first century B.C. This stretch features impressive arches that allow the aqueduct commissioned by Agrippa to cross the river Gard. The system was built to bring water to Nemausus (Nîmes) from a spring near Uzès almost fifty kilometers away.

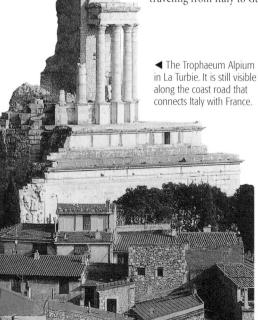

◀ The Trophaeum Alpium in La Turbie. It is still visible along the coast road that connects Italy with France.

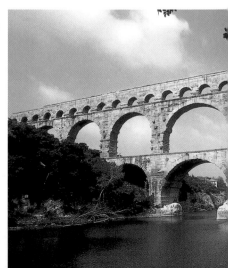

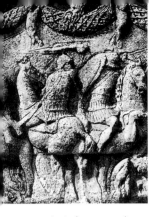

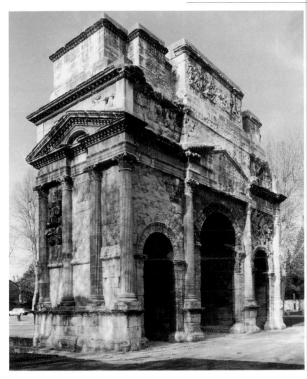

▶ An honorary arch in Orange built circa 30 B.C.–A.D. 26. The composition of the attic is unique, where reliefs stand out from the background without being framed. This technique was unknown to the Greeks and Romans but is similar to the Etruscan-Hellenistic sarcophagi in Tarquinia.

▶ The Maison Carrée in Nîmes dates to the Augustan period. The temple is still perfectly preserved to this day. It was built in the forum and dedicated to the princes Gaius and Lucius Caesar.

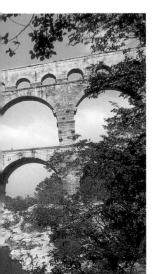

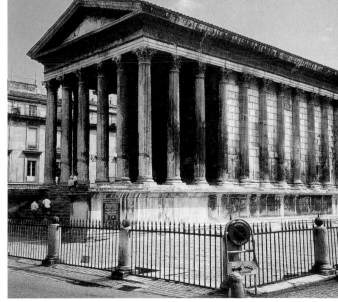

ART AND ARCHITECTURE

Portraits of the Julio-Claudian Family

Typical iconography from the Augustan period was influenced by identifying the state with the prince and by the cult of imperial personality. Augustus's interest in founding a dynasty necessarily brought with it the need to familiarize public opinion, and especially the army, with the concept of "dynasty" itself. This was also accomplished by accenting similar traits in different family members. The princes destined to succeed Augustus, such as his nephews Gaius and Lucius, were brought to resemble the emperor in behavior, in the serene expressions on their faces, and especially with identical hairstyles. So much so, in fact, that it is difficult to recognize who is who without the accompanying inscriptions. From the beginnings of the principate, portraits of the Julio-Claudian family were widely diffused in Italy and the provinces. The matching images became a way of legitimizing and transferring power. The images of the individuals tended to be stereotypical, eliminating anything that was realistic from the physical characteristics. From Augustus to Claudius, these portraits seem the work of a classical mold. Only with Nero's reign would a new baroque emphasis vigorously reemerge and create the basis for the renewed realism of the Flavian period that would follow.

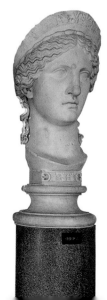

▶ Hera Ludovisi. This colossal head was identified as the protrait of Antonia Augusta, the mother of the emperor Claudius. She was divinized by her son after her death and celebrated as a supreme example of married virtue and maternal dedication. The sculpture is one of the most admired of all time and was mentioned by Goethe in his *Italian Journey 1786–1788*. Rome, Palazzo Altemps.

▲ The emperor Caligula ruled from A.D. 37 to 41 and here wears a cuirass and the Roman military cloak (*paludamentum*). Venice, Museo Archeologico.

▶ Agrippina the younger, dressed for worship. The work is made from basalt, a rare, precious, greenish-black stone from the Egyptian desert. Rome, Centrale Montemartini.

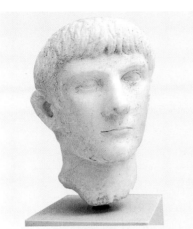

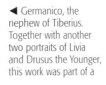

◄ Germanico, the nephew of Tiberius. Together with another two portraits of Livia and Drusus the Younger, this work was part of a statue cycle with marked provincial characteristics of ancient Asido, present-day Medina Sidon near Cádiz. Cádiz, Museo Arqueológico.

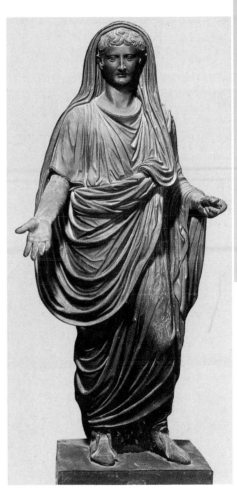

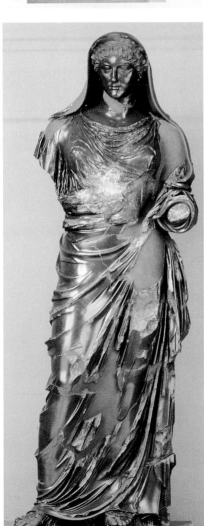

▲ A bronze statue of Tiberius, from Herculaneum. As supreme pontiff, the emperor is portrayed similarly to Augustus. The ideology of power shows itself here through an identification and adherence to republican religious tradition, abandoning the hero image of the Hellenistic dynasties. Naples, Museo Archeologico Nazionale.

Nero and the Domus Aurea

After Nero's residence, the Domus Transitoria, was destroyed in the devastating fire of A.D. 64, the emperor ordered the construction of a new, magnificent dwelling on approximately a hundred hectares of the slopes of Palatine hill. It would have daring new architecture and incredibly rich decorations. On a vault in a hall dedicated to Hector and Andromache, for instance, there are painted griffins facing each other in a complex geometric plaster pattern (see below).

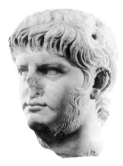

▲ Nero, from A.D. 59–64, discovered in the area of the Temple of Apollo on Palatine hill. This is perhaps one of the best portraits of the prince, characterized by a bulky head that was typical of his paternal family, the Ahenobarbi. His short beard has been partly cut into the face, and his hair is still combed across his forehead, continuing the fashion of the Julio-Claudian dynasty. Rome, Museo Palatino.

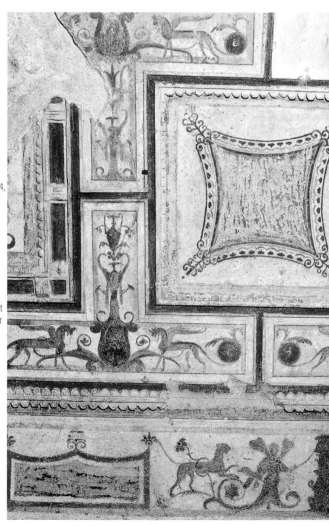

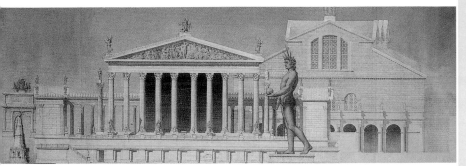

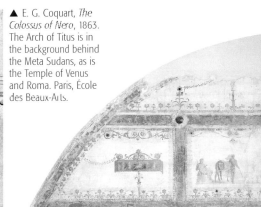

▲ E. G. Coquart, *The Colossus of Nero*, 1863. The Arch of Titus is in the background behind the Meta Sudans, as is the Temple of Venus and Roma. Paris, École des Beaux-Arts.

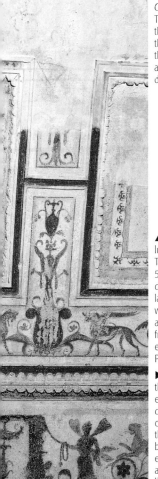

▲ A decoration from a lunette in the Domus Transitoria from A.D. 54–64. A *pinax* with open doors is above a candelabra in the left frame, while on the right there is a scene perhaps taken from one of Homer's epics. Rome, Museo Palatino.

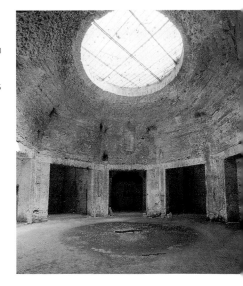

▶ An octagonal hall in the Domus Aurea. The eastern side of the residence (*domus*) has a curved rhythm to it, with the great hall covered by a dome. This was extremely innovative and anticipated the broken-lined architecture of the second century A.D.

The Flavian Dynasty: A Turning Point for the Principate

The empire was thrown into chaos in A.D. 68 when Nero was violently eliminated. For almost a century, one clan had absolutely dominated. It soon became quite clear, however, that Rome was not the only center where political decisions could be made. The Senate and magistrates represented opposing interests and only momentarily agreed to oppose Nero. After a year of bloody struggles, during which four different emperors faced off against each other, power came to rest in the hands of Vespasian. He was esteemed by many but did not come from the aristocracy, having been born in Rieti, in Sabini, into a family of the emerging classes of suburban Rome. The social and cultural figure of the new emperor and the way he came to power indicate how significant a turning point the crisis of A.D. 68–69 was for the Roman Empire. With prudent but determined politics, Vespasian succeeded in reconciling an understandable need for stability with a good dose of innovation, especially regarding the political establishment and financial institutions.

▶ *Portrait of a Lady*, from the Flavian era. Her elaborate hairstyle of curls and ringlets contrasts with the smoothness of her face that was typical of this period. Naples, Museo Archeologico Nazionale.

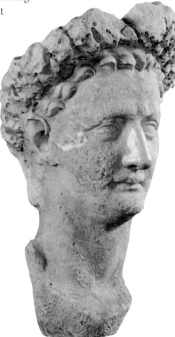

▶ Domitian wearing the civic crown. Marble portraits of the last Flavian emperor are rare, due to the fact that most were destroyed after the prince was killed. His successors cancelled out and cursed his memory (*damnatio memoriae*). Rome, Palazzo Massimo alle Terme.

▶ A private portrait of Vespasian from A.D. 69–79. With Vespasian, the distinction between official, honorary portraits and private, funerary ones was lessened, as it was in pre-Augustan times. The ruler's face, as it appears in this sculpture, fully corresponds to descriptions by historians: an aging military man from common origins who resembles a farmer. Copenhagen, Ny Carlsberg Glyptothek.

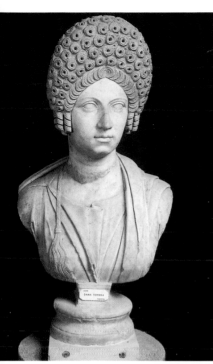

▼ *Julia of Titus*, circa A.D. 81, from an island in the Tiber River. The twelve-year-old daughter of Emperor Titus is depicted here in the year of her father's death or soon after. Rome, Palazzo Massimo alle Terme.

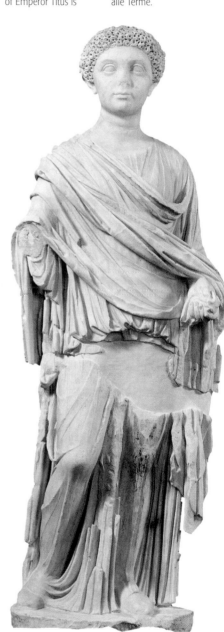

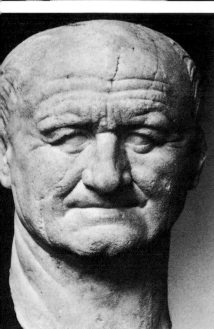

ART AND ARCHITECTURE

Flavian Art

During the reign of Claudius, and especially during Nero's time, sculpture began to disassociate itself from the influence that Athenian art had had on Augustan art. This continued with the Flavian emperors, until sculpture freed itself entirely. However, Flavian art should probably not be considered as a new and autonomous artistic tradition but rather a rekindling of Hellenistic tendencies after a tangent in the Augustan era. In the Flavian era, the relationship between audience and art changed. This was the beginning of more complex changes that a century later would bring the spectator to participate in sculptural scenes. People would gather around a circle of statues portraying characters that faced the composition's center, they themselves forming a second row. Architecture, too, reached great importance during this time, not so much for decorative forms as for new techniques that allowed new developments in how space could be organized. The great Roman art as we know it was created during this time and developed through the fourth century A.D. Hemispheric domes and cross vaults became more widespread, as did lighter items such as amphorae, which were two-handed, ceramic jugs.

▼ A stucco painting, circa A.D. 55–79, from Pompeii. This particular technique of painting a stucco relief was widespread in Pompeii after the earthquake of A.D. 62. It was primarily used in the thermal baths. Naples, Museo Archeologico Nazionale.

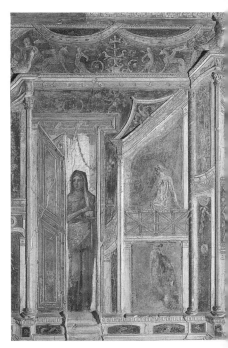

◄ A bone hairpin with one end decorated with a small female bust from the Flavian period. It was found in a burial niche in Tortona. These hairpins were used for women's hairstyles, and this one is especially refined. Turin, Museo di Antichità.

► A still life from A.D. 49–79 found in the Cervi house in Herculaneum. This scene is a part of a group of still-life paintings that are masterpieces of technique, execution, and composition. Here the painter flaunts his talents by rendering the lass transparent. Naples, Museo Archeologico Nazionale.

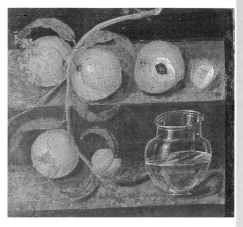

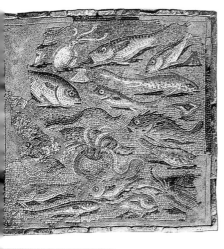

◄ A mosaic emblem of fish from Flavian-era Aquileia. The emblem is made up of stone tiles and baked into a marble background from Carrara. This was surrounded by a terra-cotta frame and inserted in an ancient mosaic floor during the late republican period. Aquileia, Museo Archeologico Nazionale.

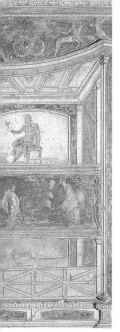

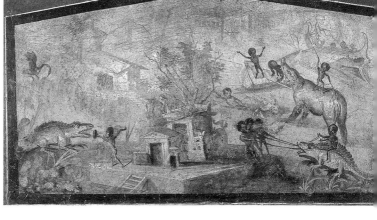

▲ A Neolithic scene, circa A.D. 55–79, from Pompeii. Together with two others, this scene was part of a decorative series in the Medico house. The main characters in the series are pygmies, who in this case are quite busy in a cruel battle with crocodiles and hippopotami.

Pompeii

In the space of a few hours between August 24 and 25, A.D. 79, Pompeii was buried under at least five or six meters of volcanic rock and ash, and Herculaneum was covered by a muddy mass of ash and water twenty meters high. Other Vesuvian towns in the area suffered a similar fate. Many people of Pompeii—although it is difficult to say exactly how many—perished in the disaster. Most suffocated from gaseous emissions from the erupting Mount Vesuvius, while others fell under the crumbling buildings. Emperor Titus formed a commission to aid the Campania area, but Pompeii had already been erased. In the course of centuries its memory was lost. When Pompeii disappeared it already had a long history, poised as it was at the mouth of a rich and productive agricultural area. The first town nucleus of Pompeii had already formed in the seventh century B.C. due to Greek and Etruscan influence, and it began to significantly expand starting in the fifth century B.C. when Samnite populations moved into the area. The major development, however, occurred after 80 B.C. when Sulla instated a colony of Roman war veterans there. In A.D. 62 a catastrophic earthquake had caused enormous damage and destruction, turning Pompeii into a huge work site of reconstruction. The water distribution reservoir of Porta Vesuvio was not yet completely restored and water had not yet reached Via dell'Abbondanza and the Stabian thermal baths when the city was surprised by the eruption.

▼ A female portrait from the end of the first century B.C., from a mosaic from Pompeii, House No. 6:15:4. This portrait of a young, jeweled woman with her hair tied back in a bun was reused for a floor in the Flavian era. Naples, Museo Archeologico Nazionale.

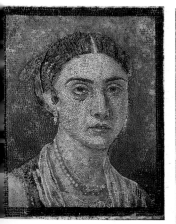

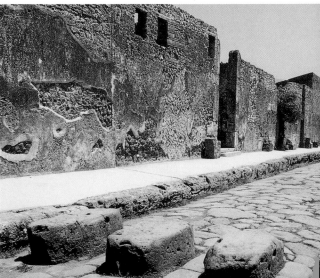

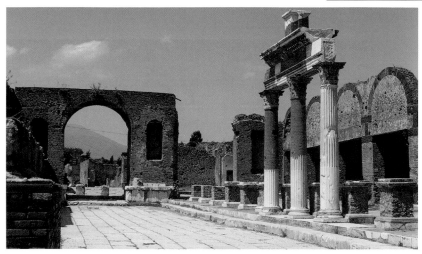

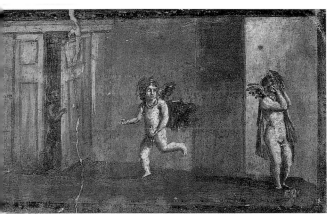

▲ The civil forum of Pompeii at the crossroads of Naples, Nola, and Stabiae (present-day Castellamare). The exteriors actually date from the second century B.C. and were resurfaced in the Julio-Claudian era.

◄ Cherubs playing hide-and-seek, circa the first half of the first century B.C., from Herculaneum. Games of skill such as hide-and-seek and blindman's bluff were often depicted on wall paintings. Naples, Museo Archeologico Nazionale.

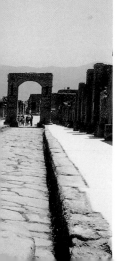

◄ Pavement and slab from the street of the forum in Pompeii. The raised blocks allowed people to cross even during heavy rains.

► A fresco of Mount Vesuvius from the Centenario house in Pompeii dating from the first half of the first century A.D. Bacchus is on the left, his whole body portrayed as a bunch of grapes. Naples, Museo Archeologico Nazionale.

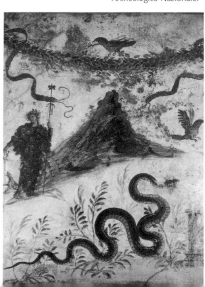

35

Styles of Pompeii

The houses of Pompeii and other Vesuvian towns are the most important sources showing how Roman painting evolved from the second century B.C. to A.D. 79. They also give witness to the Greek and Hellenistic styles that were reworked and reproduced in an Italic manner. A variety of decorative schemes, distinguished as the four Pompeian styles, became fashionable at different times. The first style, which emerged between the second century and beginning of the first century B.C., imitated stucco blocks or slabs of colored marble. In the second style, which began around 80 B.C.—when Pompeii became a Roman colony—and lasted through the Augustan period, wall decorations became more complex, providing an illusion of architectural perspectives. The third style, which can be placed from 20 B.C. to A.D. 50, linked itself to Augustan classicism. Here the element of illusion gave way to a pure reality of painting. In the fourth style, most commonly found in Pompeii because it was still in use when the city was destroyed, walls were rigidly divided in three parts with large panels and architectural representations. Here a taste for articulated and superimposed perspectives reemerged.

▶ A painting from Herculaneum in the fourth style. This design of a theatrical set is framed by a mask and curtain draping above. A central building is flanked by two, thin, lateral entranceways. In the background, which has been painted in lighter colors, a two-floor colonnade rises. Naples, Museo Archeologico Nazionale.

▼ A cup with paint color from Pompeii. The color *ceruleum* was also known as Pompeian blue or Alexandria frit. It was made from minerals and used in wall painting. Naples, Museo Archeologico Nazionale.

▼ A third-style decoration from the Agrippa Postumo a Boscotrecase villa. Multicolored, naturalistic decorations provide the frame for a large central painting of a country sanctuary on a white background. Naples, Museo Archeologico Nazionale.

▶ A decoration in the second style from Boscoreale. This architectural perspective is composed of a colonnade, with a paneled door quite visible behind it. There are hunting scenes above the doorway. Naples, Museo Archeologico Nazionale.

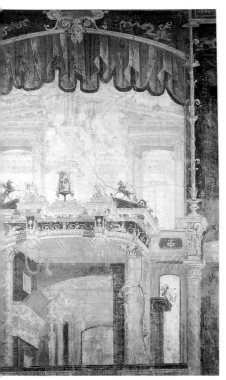

▼ A first-style decoration from a house in Pompeii. This fake door, which was probably created for reasons of symmetry, is a part of the wall of a rectangular hall. It is one of the most complete examples of the first style. The last inhabitant of the house, Julius Polybius, covered its façade and one of the entrances with electoral posters with his name on them.

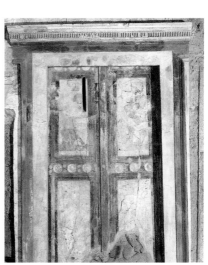

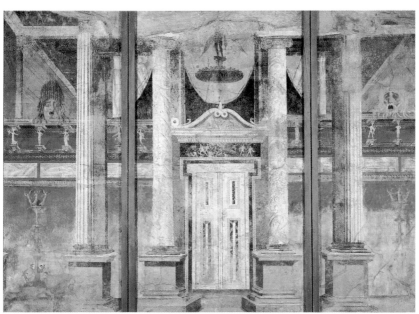

27 B.C.–A.D. 96

The Arch of Titus and the Historic Roman Relief

A white marble arch was built in honor of Titus's exploits in Judea and dominates the Roman Forum. The two huge internal panels describe the triumphal parade in Rome in A.D. 71 that celebrated the conquest of Jerusalem the year before. All the defining characteristics of the typical Roman historic relief are here: the figures are packed together, and the relief gradually diminishes in depth from the almost completely round horse heads to the flattened heads and spears of the background.

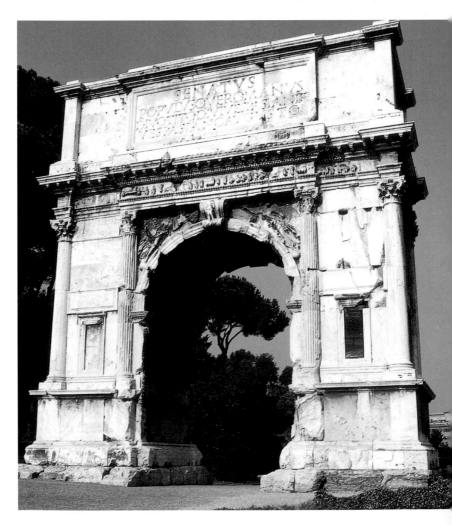

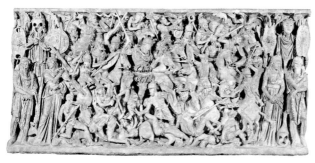

◀ A sarcophagus from Portonaccio, circa A.D. 180. This is a battle scene between Romans and barbarians. According to a hierarchical perspective, the Roman general, who throws himself into the mix on horseback, is larger than the other characters. Rome, Palazzo Massimo alle Terme.

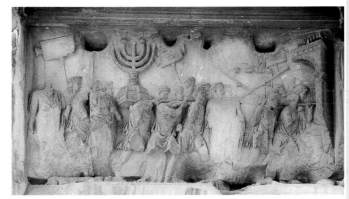

▶ Looting the temple in Jerusalem, from the Arch of Titus in Rome. The triumphal parade is shown on the left panel. A group of servants carries the sacred furnishings of the temple including a menorah, symbol of the Jewish faith. The entire population of Rome attended the parade, crowding both sides to see.

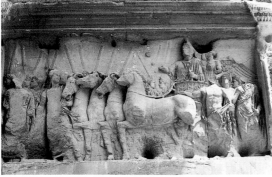

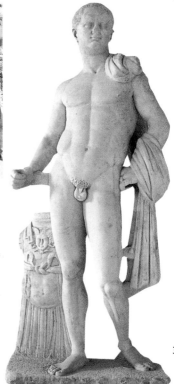

▲ The emperor's four-horse chariot, or quadriga, from the Arch of Titus in Rome. Titus, who in reality was celebrating the triumph together with his father, Vespasian, stands on the chariot and is crowned by the wings of victory while Valor (*Vitrus*) accompanies him on foot.

▶ Titus, from the Aragonese Castle in Baia, Bacoli, Naples. The larger-than-life features of the statue give the emperor a stance that recalls the republican period.

Bread and Circuses

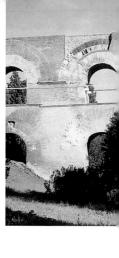

One of the many measures adopted in order to improve the quality of city life during the first imperial age (the "bread" of "bread and circuses") was to guarantee the water supply. The impressive structures of the aqueducts and their unmistakable presence in the countryside became an emblem of the new imperial order. In Rome the entire water system was expanded, and every day more than a million cubic meters of water flowed into the city, a quantity that would only be matched in recent decades. Even the smaller cities, whether in Italy or the provinces, had no need to envy the capital. Between the Augustan and Flavian eras the largest public entertainment venues were also built (for the "circuses"), such as the Colosseum and the arenas in Pola, Croatia, and Verona. There was the Theater of Marcellus in Rome and another theater in Orange. Statues of the imperial family, local authorities, and divine protectors were placed on the façades of the theaters. The amphitheater games depended on the generosity of the emperor and magistrates who sponsored them, and spectators were continually exposed to the hierarchy and political propaganda.

▼ The Theater of Marcellus was commissioned by Caesar and completed by Augustus, who dedicated it to his nephew and inaugurated it with sumptuous games in A.D. 13. The front of the audience seating is still visible today, having been used as the foundation for Palazzo Orsini during the Renaissance.

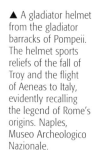

▲ A gladiator helmet from the gladiator barracks of Pompeii. The helmet sports reliefs of the fall of Troy and the flight of Aeneas to Italy, evidently recalling the legend of Rome's origins. Naples, Museo Archeologico Nazionale.

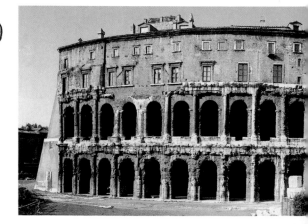

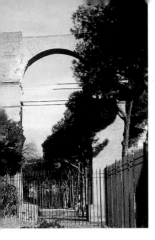

◄ A section of the Claudian-Neronian aqueduct. It was begun by Caligula in A.D. 38 and finished by Claudius in A.D. 52. Water from springs in Subiaco reached Rome through the aqueduct's sixty-eight kilometers, sixteen of which were made up of tufa block arches. Today the arches are still partly visible in the countryside.

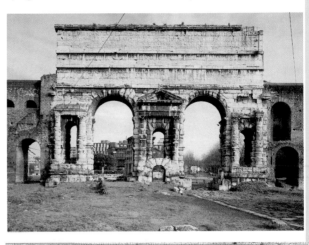

► Porta Maggiore. Claudius built the monumental double arch at Rome's entrance. It bridged the gap between Via Prenestina and Via Labicana and is a visible element of the Claudian-Neronian aqueduct.

► A mosaic of a satirical choir from the House of the Tragic Poet in Pompeii, circa A.D. 62–79. The actors prepare for the show, and their masks lie on the ground and on the shelf to the right. Naples, Museo Archeologico Nazionale.

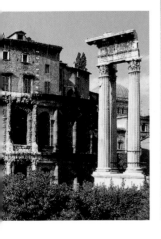

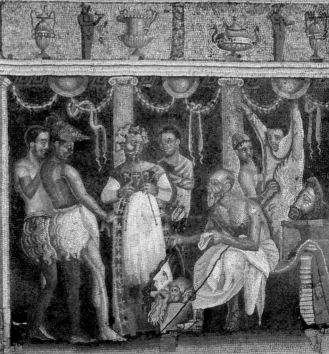

MASTERPIECES OF ART

The Colosseum

Rome's first permanent amphitheater was commissioned by Vespasian in the area that had previously hosted the imperial residence, the Domus Aurea. The Colosseum was inaugurated by Titus in A.D. 80 with a hundred days of games. The imposing structure, laid out as an ellipse, was able to accommodate as many as fifty thousand people on its three floors of tiers. An immense awning covered the entire building and was maneuvered into position by sailors from the fleet at Misenum. Gladiator contests were held at the Colosseum until they were prohibited in A.D. 404, and hunting shows continued through A.D. 523.

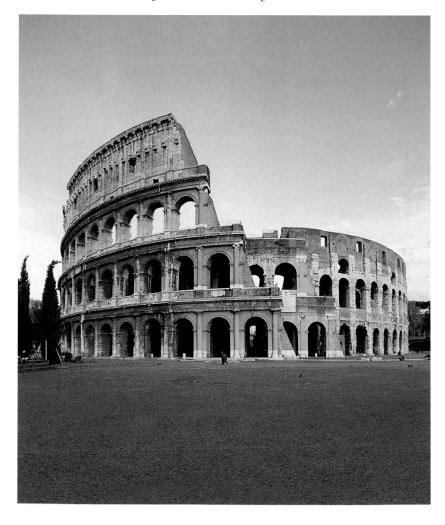

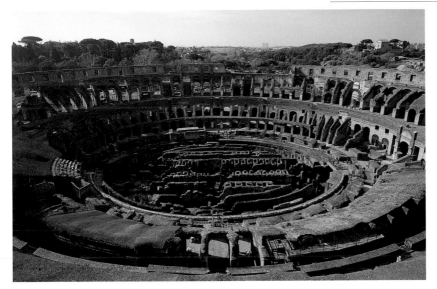

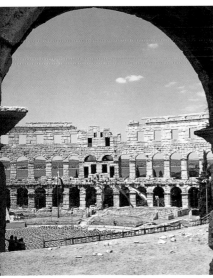

◄ The amphitheater in Pola, Croatia, built during the Flavian period. This is a view of the amphitheater's interior through one of the arches. This venue could hold more than twenty thousand spectators and was built with two floors of arches made from rock from Istria that has survived well to this day.

▲ A view of the Colosseum's interior. The arena floor was covered by wooden boards that hid a dense series of tunnels from the audience's view. These were used for storing sets, hid a series of lifts, and allowed wild animals to enter the arena.

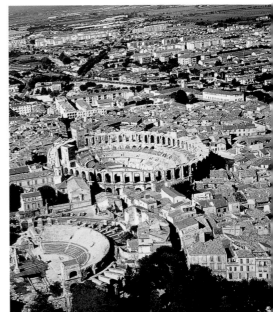

► Arles, France. In this aerial view of the city, the theater and the amphitheater that date to the Flavian period are recognizable, but are away from where the ancient center of the city originally was. They are still used today for bullfights. Like the Colosseum, the amphitheater at Arles was transformed numerous times during the course of the centuries, thanks to its easily fortified structure. Prints, drawings, and watercolors show that houses were built in the audience seating area.

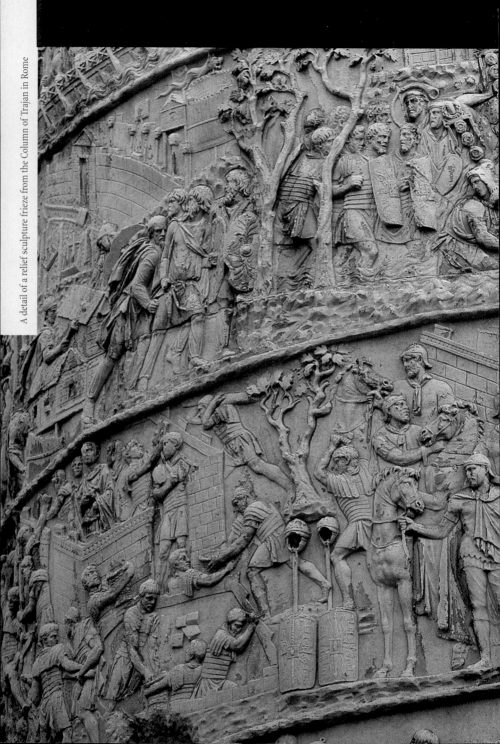

A detail of a relief sculpture frieze from the Column of Trajan in Rome

The Height of the Empire:
From Trajan to the Antonines

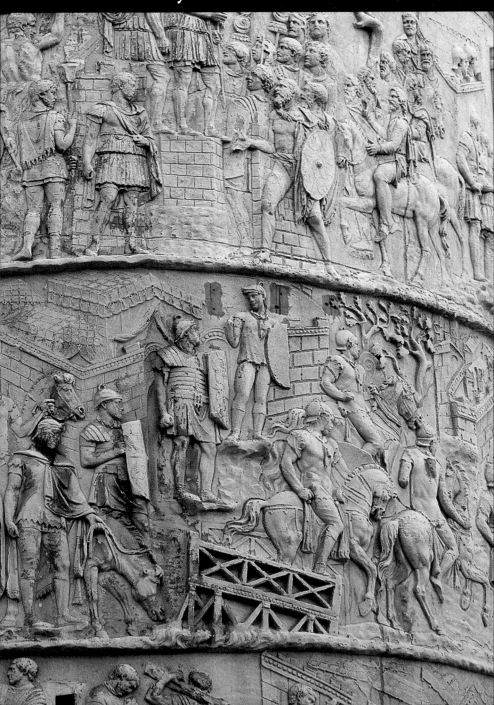

Trajan the *Optimus Princeps*

▶ A sesterce coin from A.D. 114 with the Column of Trajan and the legend *Optimo Princips*. The idea of depicting public buildings on coins had political importance and was quite common. Bucharest, Muzeul de Istorie a Romanici.

The last emperor of the Flavian dynasty, Domitian, was assassinated after a palace conspiracy in A.D. 96, and an aged senator, Cocceio Nerva, was placed on the throne. In a stroke of political genius, Nerva chose an energetic general to succeed him. Marcus Ulpius Trajanus was commander of the troops that were stationed in Germany. This was a new way to manage power, and it allowed the emperor to maintain good relations with the Roman Senate while at the same time remaining the true arbitrator of the political scene. For almost a century, imperial succession would be regulated by the prince, who would choose his successor. At the end of Nerva's short, two-year reign, Trajan was in Germany, and it seems that his power was so established that his presence in Rome was not even required in order to sanction his succession. The new sovereign—the first of non-Italic origin—was born in Italica, Spain, into an aristocratic, Hispanic, provincial family. They had earned their right to be a part of the ruling class of the empire. The Roman Senate bestowed the title *optimus princeps* on Trajan in A.D. 114 after he had ruled more than fourteen years. This was far beyond the title Octavian had given himself a century and a half earlier. "Augustus" was a greeting with a tinge of religious halo; "best prince" was instead given to someone who had governed with discipline, honesty, and intelligence. The sovereign was the first civil servant, defending and enlarging the borders of the empire until they reached their maximum expansion.

▲ Plotina, circa A.D. 112-122, from the cold room (*frigidarium*) at the Thermal Baths of Neptune in Ostia. Trajan's wife is portrayed here as having a mature age. She was not often depicted during her life, and was celebrated and divinized by Hadrian. Rome, Palazzo Massimo alle Terme.

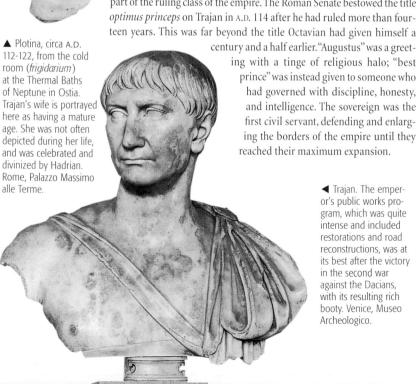

◀ Trajan. The emperor's public works program, which was quite intense and included restorations and road reconstructions, was at its best after the victory in the second war against the Dacians, with its resulting rich booty. Venice, Museo Archeologico.

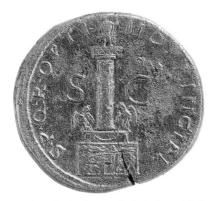

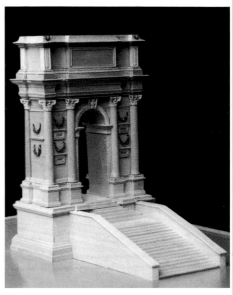

▼ The Arch of Trajan in Benevento, built in A.D. 114. The reliefs of the arch illustrate scenes of peace on the city side and war scenes on the side facing the countryside.

▶ A plastic model of the arch built in Trajan's honor near the port of Ancona. The emperor embarked on his conquest of Dacia from that city. Ancona, Instituto d'Arte.

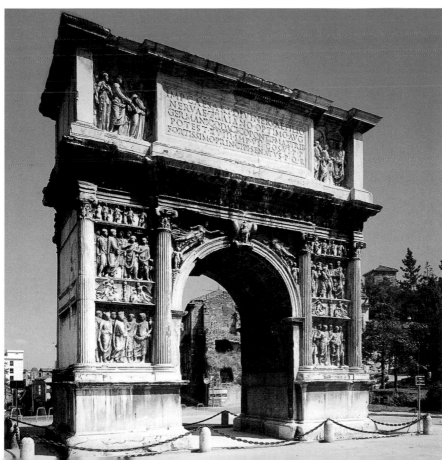

The Trajan Forum and Market

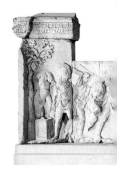

The Trajan Forum—the most impressive of all the imperial forums—was built between A.D. 107 and 113, thanks to financial resources from the recent conquest of Dacia. The architect for the project, Apollodorus of Damascus, was the most celebrated architect of the time. In order to find the necessary space in the built-up area between the Roman Forum and the surrounding hills, he was forced to dig up the saddle connecting Quirinal hill with Capitoline hill. At the center of the huge, three-hundred-meter-long square stood a statue of Trajan on horseback, while the Ulpia Basilica rose above the northern side. Behind it a column stood between two celebrated public libraries, one for Greek writings, the other for Latin. Various volumes were stored inside in wooden chests that were inserted into niches still visible today. A great brick complex was built to the sides of the forum for commercial uses. There was a series of multi-level boutiques that opened onto Via Biberatica, which went up the hill from the forum. The emperor requested the impressive market probably to guarantee the proper management of grain shipments and other goods that reached Rome through the new port at Fiumicino. The Trajan Forum was the center of Roman life for quite a while, and even in the fourth century A.D. it had kept all its splendor.

▲ *Pluteo di Traiano*, (Trajan's Shelter). This is a scene of conditional amnesty for tax evaders and a destruction of debt records. In the background, monuments from the Roman Forum are recognizable. Rome, Curia Giulia.

▶ The principal events concerning Trajan's two campaigns against the Dacians are told in 155 frames of reliefs.

◀ This is a reconstruction of one of Trajan's trophies in Adamklissi, Romania. It was built circa A.D. 109 on the Black Sea to celebrate his victory against the Dacians.

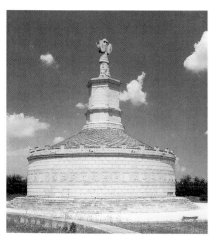

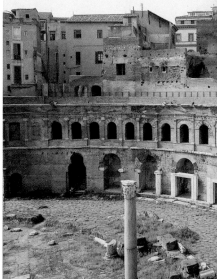

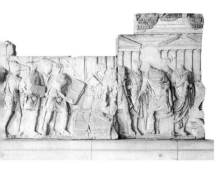

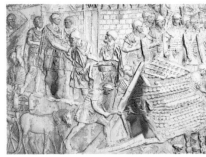

▼ The Trajan Market in Rome. The northern half of the large semicircle is shown here with the road that separates it from the eastern side of the forum. The standing column belongs to the quadrangular area of the forum floor.

▶ The Trajan Column in Rome. Built of large marble blocks from Luni, the column was initially intended as a measurement recalling how high the original hills in the area were after they were leveled in order to build the new forum.

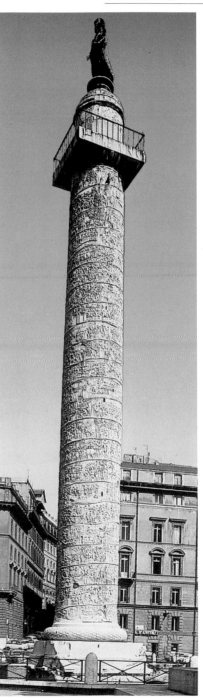

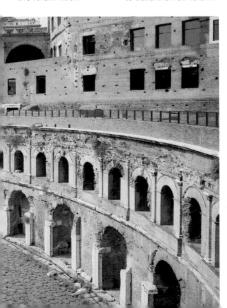

The Provinces: Hispania

The Roman conquest of the Iberian Peninsula began very early. During the second Punic War (218–201 B.C.), the southwest side of the peninsula (Hispania Ulterior) was partly brought under the influence of Rome. The conquest of Lusitania—modern-day Portugal—was soon to follow. Roman art from Hispania is very different from the other western provinces, probably because of this early contact with Rome and the many other contacts the Spanish had with Greeks and Phoenicians through commerce. So the dominant Iberian class—already soaked by Hellenism—absorbed the official Roman art better than other peoples. This left little room for art that was truly provincial. The people of Hispania were especially interested in works of bronze, tableware, equestrian decorations, and miniature statues. The presence of copper mines was taken advantage of since ancient times and must have spurred on local or temporary shops for bronze artisans. The territories of the peninsula were mostly well off—Pliny, in fact, tells how Hispania was even richer than Gaul in the first century—thanks to gold, iron, and tin deposits and the production of oil, wine, and other exportable goods. Economically depressed areas, recounts Pliny, furnished unskilled labor.

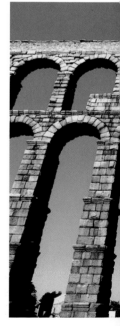

▼ An aqueduct near Segovia from the first century A.D. The imposing arches still cross the city today. The Romans were extremely careful in maintaining their water system. Augustus created a public office, the *cura aquarum*, to be in charge of inspecting the aqueducts.

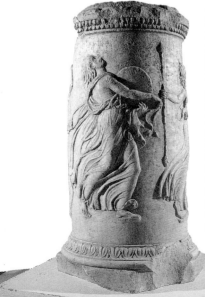

◄ A cylindrical altar from the end of the Augustan period. The relief shows a parade of worshippers who dance in honor of Dionysos. The figures are arranged in rigorous sequence and are all positioned in a straight line. The altar is from the theater in Italica and was together with two others showing similar scenes, although the others showed couples and featured a satyr among them. Seville, Museo Arqueológico Provincial.

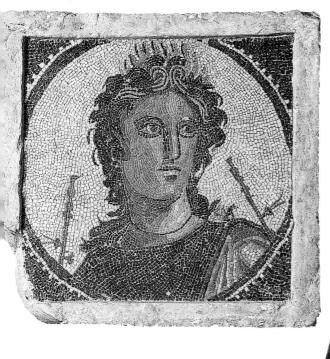

◀ A mosaic of Euterpe, circa A.D. 150–175, from the Roman villa of Els Munts in Altafulla, Tarragona, Spain. This multicolored mosaic, together with others, was created with tiny tiles placed on a brick backing. Tarragona, Museu Nacional Arqueològic.

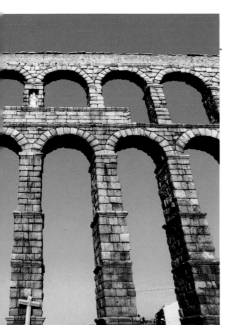

▶ A lamp holder (*lampadophor*) from the first century A.D. This bronze statue, which measures about eighty centimeters high, portrays an African child standing and bringing a tray. A tiny oil lamp was placed on the tray along with a wick, with bronze tweezers to adjust it. Tarragona, Museu Nacional Arqueològic.

51

Hadrian's Villa

The Canopus (see below), a lily pool with columns and statues, is one of the most notable and monumental features of the extravagant residence that Hadrian built at the edge of Rome. It became a luxury vacation spot for the emperor during his brief stays there.

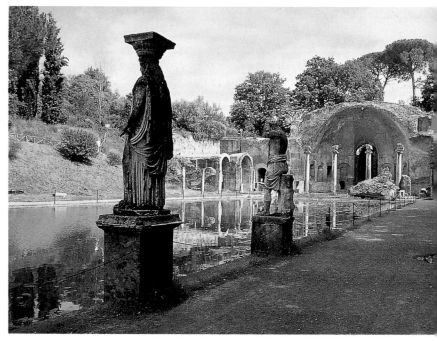

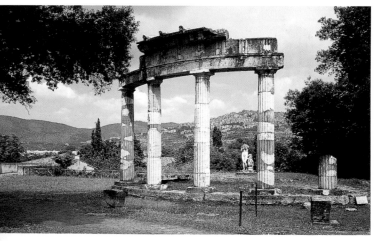

◀ A northeast view of the Doric temple. Although Hadrian spent much of his time as emperor outside of Italy, he still attempted to achieve his ideals of an architecture that recalled the ancient Greek world and built an imperial residence worthy of the imperial court's splendor. These evocative ruins of the villa can still be admired today in a vast area on the slopes where Tivoli eventually emerged.

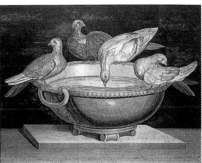

◀ A mosaic depicting doves from Hadrian's villa. This is a multicolored emblem with leafy decorations and a white background. The picture, a copy of a celebrated Hellenistic work by the artist Sosos of Pergamum, illustrates Hadrian's tastes for copying and re-elaborating older works. Rome, Musei Capitolini.

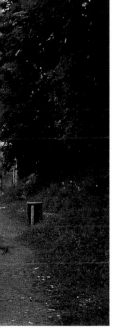

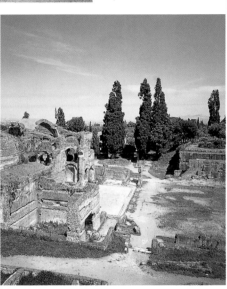

▶ A northwest view of the back courtyard and the eastern part of the thermal baths. North of the Canopus was the seaside complex of small and large baths, which had a traditional water system. The ceilings were vaulted and can still be partially seen today. This was quite advanced and complex for that period.

▼ Hadrian's Villa reaches an area of about three hundred hectares. It includes different groups of buildings, each one with its own specific and functional characteristics.

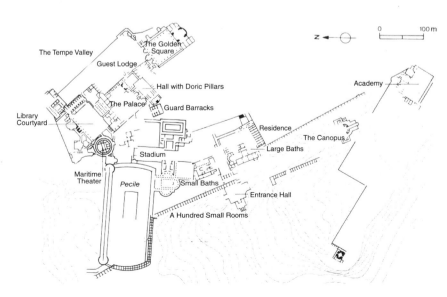

The Tempe Valley
The Golden Square
Guest Lodge
Hall with Doric Pillars
Academy
The Palace
Guard Barracks
Library Courtyard
Residence
The Canopus
Stadium
Large Baths
Maritime Theater
Pecile
Small Baths
Entrance Hall
A Hundred Small Rooms

0   100 m

Hadrian and Antinous

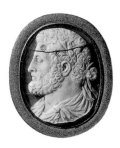

Antinous was a young man whom Hadrian loved and made his favorite, showering him with honors. He was born around A.D. 110 in Bithynia, a region of modern-day Turkey on the Black Sea. During a visit to Egypt with the emperor in A.D. 130, Antinous mysteriously drowned in the Nile and was subsequently transformed into a deity. Perhaps it was an accident, but there was also talk of ritual suicide that Antinous supposedly performed in order to save Hadrian from misfortunes that an astrologer had predicted. The emperor was deeply upset by the loss of his favorite and founded the city of Antinoöpolis near where Antinous died in order to honor his memory. He also credited stories that said a new star had appeared in the heavens, and so Antinous's spirit became a god. His worship spread mostly in the eastern provinces of the empire. In Rome, too, an obelisk was erected. (Today it is at Pincio, in Rome.) Surviving statues of Antinous sometimes portray him as Osiris, Adonis, or Dionysos, and in one relief from a private collection he appears as the god Silvanus. All these depictions date to the brief span of time between Antinous's death and Hadrian's. The short-lived devotion to Antinous did not survive beyond the emperor's life.

▼ Antinous, circa A.D. 130–134. This is the only bronze portrait that has survived and dates, together with other replicas, to an original from Athens. It imitated the great Greek statues. Florence, Museo Archeologico Nazionale.

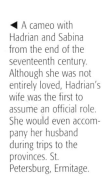

◄ A cameo with Hadrian and Sabina from the end of the seventeenth century. Although she was not entirely loved, Hadrian's wife was the first to assume an official role. She would even accompany her husband during trips to the provinces. St. Petersburg, Ermitage.

◄ A two-layered onyx cameo of Hadrian from the second century A.D. The gold mounting dates to the beginning of the nineteenth century. St. Petersburg, Ermitage.

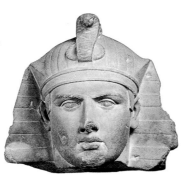

◄ The head of Antinous as Osiris. This red-marble statue possibly belongs to a group of four showing Antinous as Osiris. The works were placed in Hadrian's villa in the Temple of Sarapis, who was an Egyptian god of the dead seen in Rome as similar to Jove. Dresden, Staatliche Kunstsammlungen.

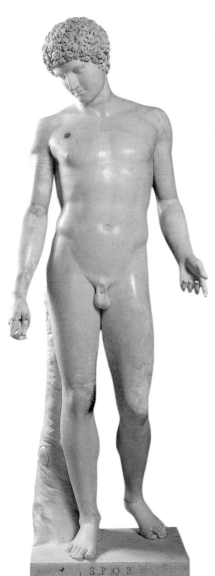

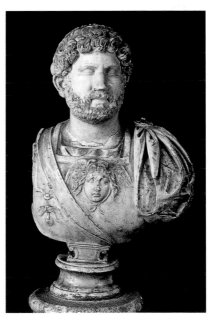

◄ *Antinous Albani.* As a typical creation from this period, this sculpture certainly represents the typical Antinous. For the last time in antiquity an artist—who was almost certainly Greek— independently placed a nude, masculine body before everyone. Rome, Musei Capitolini.

▲ A bust of Hadrian. He became part of Trajan's family (the emperor had no heir) thanks to his paternal grandfather's marriage to one of the emperor's aunts. Seville, Museo Arqueológico.

ART AND ARCHITECTURE

Urban and Architectural Development

Many cities of the empire were embellished and enriched with monuments and public works during Hadrian's rule, and today there are archeological traces of many of these. In Athens a magnificent library with a hundred columns of *pavonazzetto* marble was built. The Olympieum was also completed there, the great temple dedicated to Zeus that had been ordered by Antiochus Epiphanes of Syria in the second century B.C. but had never been finished. The emperor ordered many architectural works in Rome. Between A.D. 118 and 125—dates that can be seen from the builders' marks on the bricks—the Pantheon of Agrippa was rebuilt, modifying the entire primitive construction. In A.D. 121 construction began on the great, two-roomed temple dedicated to Venus and Roma built on a man-made platform. The emperor himself was the author of the project. On the banks of the Tiber, Hadrian had a mausoleum for himself and for his successors erected, modeled after Augustus's sepulcher. He connected the city with a new bridge that is still being used to this day, the Elio. Above all, however, it seems the emperor's architectural passions found a free outlet when he built his villa near Tivoli. It was meant to recall the most famous monuments from the Greek and eastern provinces of the empire while at the same time using technical and innovative solutions.

▼ The Pantheon in Rome. The eight monolithic columns are made of pink and gray blocks of Egyptian granite with white marble capitals and bases. The two left columns were taken down during the Middle Ages and replaced in the seventeenth century using columns from Nero's thermal baths.

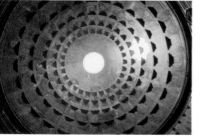

▲ The interior of the Pantheon's dome. The dome was made of a single cement cast above an immense wooden structure. With a diameter of over forty-three meters, it is the largest masonry dome ever created. The interior is decorated with five levels of concentric frames.

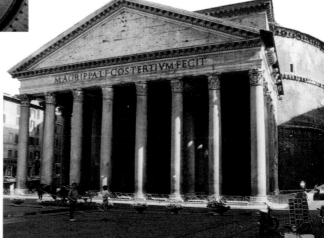

MAGRIPPALFCOSTERTIVMFECIT

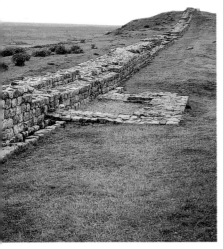

◄ Hadrian's ramparts in Great Britain. The British Isles were not easy to govern. After Caesar disembarked in 55 B.C., Claudius eventually conquered them. In order to keep hostile tribes from Scotland outside the boundaries of the empire, Hadrian ordered construction of a defensive structure that cut the island in two. The wall had look-out towers and a deep moat.

▼ Castel Sant'Angelo in Rome. Hadrian's mausoleum was trans- formed into a fort as early as the fourth cen- tury A.D. It later became the cornerstone of the Vatican's defense system during the Middle Ages as well as a prison. Later changes saw the original ornamentation and marble removed, until the castle assumed its present name during the Renaissance.

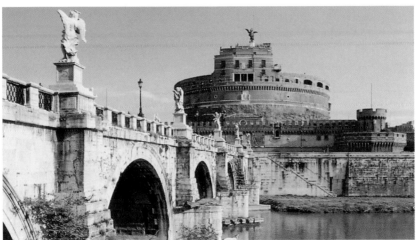

▶ The Temple of Venus and Roma in Rome. The monumental ruins of the temple are still visible on the slopes of Velia hill that face the Colosseum. The vault dates to Maxentius's restoration. In order to construct the building Hadrian demolished the entrance hall to the Domus Aurea and removed the *Colossus*— the enormous statue inside—using a wagon towed by twenty-four elephants.

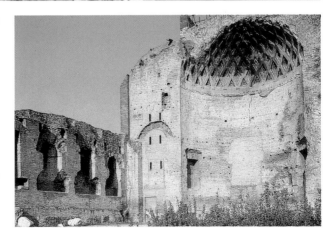

Palmyra

The oasis of Palmyra in Syria long enjoyed a certain independence. It had become a Roman colony during the reign of Septimius Severus but was destroyed in A.D. 273 after having dominated the eastern part of the empire for a brief time.

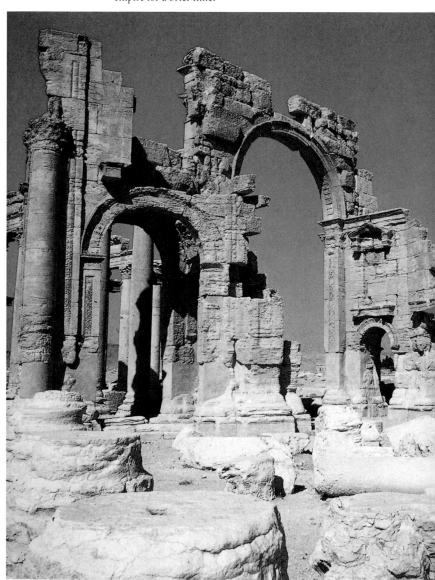

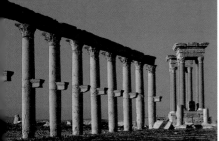

◀ During the imperial period, Palmyra, "city of the palms," became a blossoming center thanks to caravans of luxurious goods that passed through. The road across the desert connected Syria to Mesopotamia and the Persian Gulf, where sea routes to India began.

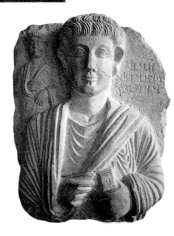

◀ A young man's tombstone from the second century B.C. in Palmyra. Cemeteries surround the city. One in the western section is called "valley of the tombs" and has rich and curious tombs that seem Iranian in their towerlike shapes. Since they held entire floors of burial recesses, these towers could hold as many as four hundred corpses.

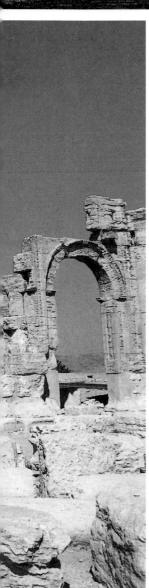

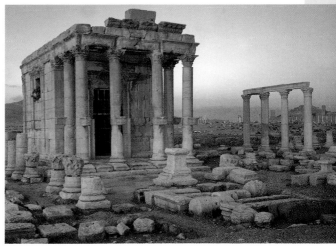

▲ The Ba'alshamin Temple in Palmyra. Hadrian's visit in A.D. 129 was an important moment for Palmyra and was certainly celebrated with splendor. One rich businessman from the city, taking on the costs himself, erected the Ba'alshamin Temple. It was built over an existing sanctuary, a place of worship for one of the city's tribes.

The Eastern Rites: Isis

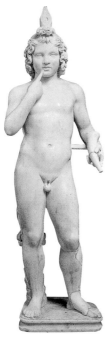

The goddess Isis, together with her husband, Osiris, and her little son, Horus (or Harpocrates), was already worshiped in the ancient Egypt of the pharaohs, and devotion to her also became popular in the Roman era as well. The goddess symbolizes the exaltation of married and maternal love. According to legend she gave birth after a long journey through Egypt collecting the dismembered pieces of her husband's body. (He had suffered this fate at the hands of his treacherous brother Seth.) She is usually portrayed as a young woman wearing a tunic that is tied at the center of her breast and holding some typical object such as the sistrum, a musical instrument similar to a small rattle. This instrument was used to animate dances at sacred ceremonies. The cult of Isis was already popular in the republican period, although for a long time it was "held hostage" by members of the aristocracy who were against introducing foreign gods into Roman society. After Egypt was conquered in 31 B.C., however, Egyptian culture and religion entered into all the social classes. Under Domitian the Temple of Isis in Rome's Campus Martius was rebuilt, and in the second century A.D. images of Isis and Horus permeated society even more thanks to Hadrian's encouragement. Devotion to Mithras also was popular during this time. This Indian-Iranian god of light was surely promoted by soldiers and merchants who were in frequent contact with the East. This cult, however, was reserved only for men who had undergone certain initiation rites.

▲ A statue of Horus from Hadrian's Villa. It portrays the young son of Isis and Osiris. His hair is traditionally tied in a knot above his forehead, and he is in a typical stance of an infant with his index finger pointing to his mouth. Rome, Musei Capitolini.

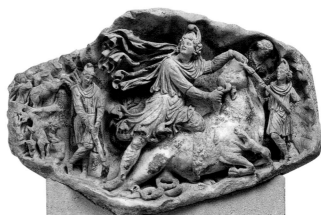

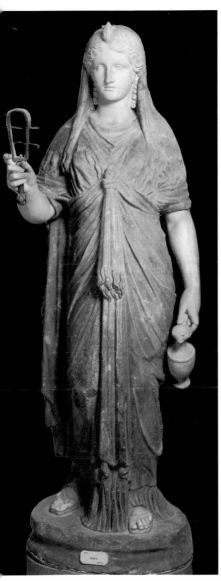

◀ A statue of Isis from the second century A.D. made from black marble with white marble for the face, arms, and feet. It is important but not unusual evidence of public devotion to Isis in Naples. Naples, Museo Archeologico Nazionale.

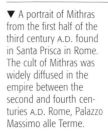

▼ A portrait of Mithras from the first half of the third century A.D. found in Santa Prisca in Rome. The cult of Mithras was widely diffused in the empire between the second and fourth centuries A.D. Rome, Palazzo Massimo alle Terme.

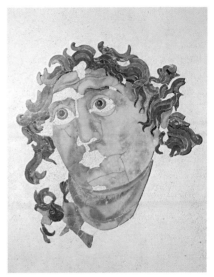

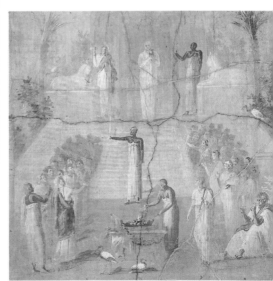

◀ Mithras killing the bull, from the second century A.D. in Aquileia. Places of worship, often underground, recalled the grotto where the god captured the bull. Vienna, Kunsthistorisches Museum.

▶ A ceremony for Isis from the middle of the first century A.D. In the center is a priest with his head shaved, dressed in a typical costume of white linen. Naples, Museo Archeologico Nazionale.

ART AND ARCHITECTURE

Marble Funeral Monuments and Sarcophagi

During this era burying the dead became more and more important and frequent, instead of the previous custom of cremation that had been used at times for hygienic purposes. Because of this, marble sarcophagi became more widely popular and were decorated with reliefs that were created by specialized shops in Rome, Athens, and Asia Minor. Fashions for sarcophagi were surely influenced by exposure to the East, where sepulchers had been used since ancient times. Progressive tendencies by Roman culture toward expressing historical and philosophical symbols on funeral monuments also supported these currents. One popular subject was the myth of Alcestes, a wife who chose to die in her husband's place and was brought back to life by Hercules. There was also that of Orestes, who sought revenge for his father by killing his mother Clytemnestra and her lover Aegisthus. Another recurring theme that also appeared in public works of the time such as arches or columns were war scenes and military activity in general. These were often found in ancient "cartoons," which expressed the fashions and hairstyles of the time. The unfinished face of the general pictured in the extremely rich and detailed sarcophagus from Portonaccio illustrates clearly how these works were a series produced by a workshop. Each would eventually be completed with the face of the deceased.

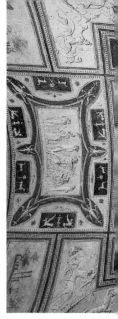

▼ Reliefs from the short ends of the sarcophagus at Portonaccio, circa A.D. 180. They depict a commander from the war that Marcus Aurelius declared against Quadi and Marcomanni. The barbarians are portrayed as peoples from the northern borders of the empire. Rome, Palazzo Massimo alle Terme.

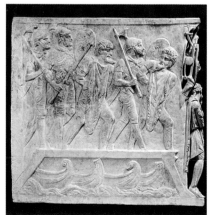

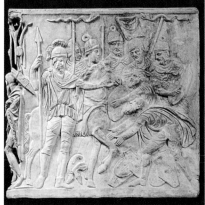

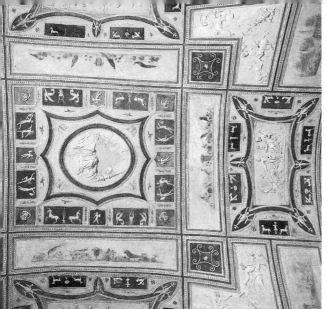

◄ A stucco vault from the tomb of the Pancrazi family on Via Latina in Rome, circa A.D. 160. In the central medallion Jove's eagle appears to carry Ganymede off to heaven. The latter was the son of the king of Troy and became cupbearer to the gods.

▼ A sarcophagus with a battle scene between the Romans and Galatians, circa A.D. 160–170. The Galatians pictured on sarcophagi from this period do not represent a specific people, but rather generic, non-Roman enemies. Rome, Musei Capitolini.

▼ A sarcophagus with the Muses, circa A.D. 140. The nine daughters of Zeus and Mnemosyne, the goddesses of poetry, art, and intellectual endeavors in general, are all celebrated as givers of the purifying force of music, poetic inspiration, and divine wisdom. Paris, Louvre.

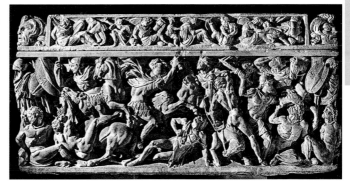

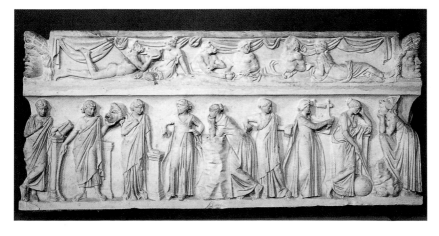

Mosaics and Stuccowork

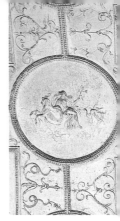

During the second century A.D. decorating floors with mosaics of black tiles on white backgrounds became quite popular in the capital and quickly spread to the suburbs and provinces. These were placed alongside other more common, geometric mosaics created using similar techniques. An interesting variety of these can be seen in the buildings of Ostia, which is one of the best-preserved areas after Rome. They allow the viewer to follow the principal lines of development and the different techniques involved in creating mosaics, which gradually included colored tiles as well. During the Antonine period, and especially in the second half of the second century A.D., a baroque taste began to emerge, which reached its fullest expression with the bust of Commodus as Hercules (page 73). In line with these transformations, decorations in painted stucco were also especially appreciated during this time. They were often quite expensive, such as those at the Pancrazi family tomb. At the tomb there are facings with imaginary architecture alternating with mythological scenes that allude to the afterlife. The decorations achieve a notable vivacity and a solemn effect at the same time. However, it is already possible to see these weightier baroque effects and color contrasts in some ceilings of the Domus Aurea—in contrast to the refined stuccowork of the Augustan period—which foreshadowed these turning points of the second century A.D.

▲ A stucco vault in the so-called Bianca tomb on Via Latina in Rome, circa A.D. 160. The background for the decoration is an intricate geometric scheme.

▶ A floor mosaic from the second century A.D. The decorative motif is a shield–stylized in this case–decorated with scales. At its center rests the head of Medusa with her repugnant head and hair of snakes. With just one look, she could turn anything to stone. Rome, Palazzo Massimo alle Terme.

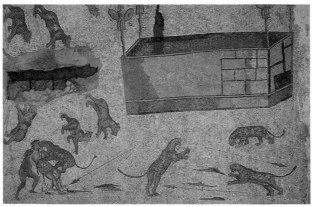

◀ A mosaic depicting capital punishment from the end of the second or beginning of the third century A.D. The first execution by wild animals was in A.D. 167, when Aemilius Paullus had foreign deserters of the Roman army trampled by elephants after the victory over Perseus of Macedonia. El Djem, Tunisia, Museo.

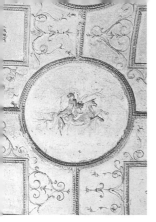

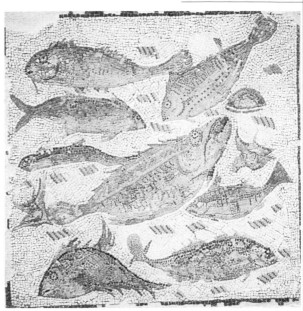

▶ A mosaic of fish, circa A.D. 117–192. This decoration was part of the floor of a country villa north of Rome, together with another thirty-one frames of different subject matter. Rome, Palazzo Massimo alle Terme.

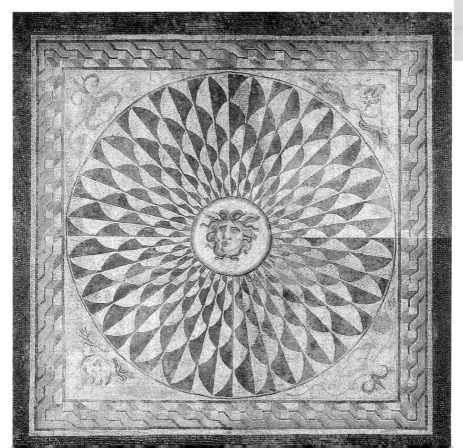

A Golden Age of Justice and Well-being

Since Hadrian's reign, contemporaries of the emperor had already defined that age of the principate as a golden one because of the balance in the political, civil, and cultural arenas. When Antoninus Pius—who although he was from Gaul, was extremely tied to Italic traditions—ascended the throne, the empire began a long period of peace. It had never known such a time and would live to regret it. His reign, mostly remembered for its progress toward more humanitarian legislation, prudent economic management, and a blossoming of education, has been defined as a period of conservatism. The Roman state was actually committed to maintaining a condition of widespread prosperity and tranquility that was the direct result of preceding conquests. Underneath, however, the propelling spirit of the empire was suffering symptoms of exhaustion, and this exceptional period of stability was hiding the beginnings of a great crisis that would explode a few decades later, despite attempts to keep it at bay by recalling the values of the great Roman tradition.

▼ A silver mirror from the second century A.D. In the relief Helle is brought to safety by the ram of the golden fleece yet falls into the sea in a place that will take her name and call itself Ellesponto. Rome, Palazzo Massimo alle Terme.

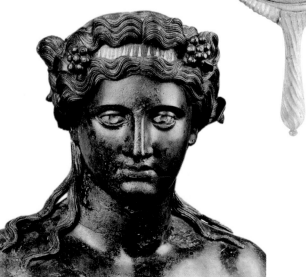

◀ A statue of Dionysos from the second century A.D. This bronze statue was derived from a model that Greek artists created toward the middle of the fourth century B.C. More than twenty copies and variations of it are known to this day. Rome, Palazzo Massimo alle Terme.

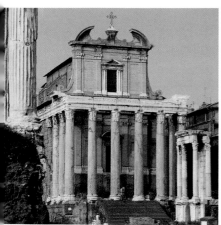

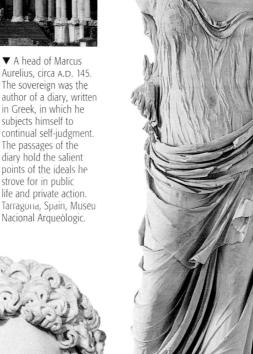

▼ A statue of Aphrodite in the so-called Hera Borgese style from the second century A.D. It is a marble copy from the Antonine period of a Greek original that was probably made at the end of the fifth century B.C. The remaining curls of hair that fall on the figure's neck lead one to think that the head of an empress must have been originally placed on the statue. Rome, Museo Palatino.

▲ The Temple of Antoninus and Faustina in the Roman Forum. Antoninus Pius erected the temple for his wife, who died in A.D. 141 and was made a goddess. The dedication of the temple to the emperor happened after his death. The building is well preserved thanks to its being transformed into the Church of San Lorenzo in Miranda.

▼ A head of Marcus Aurelius, circa A.D. 145. The sovereign was the author of a diary, written in Greek, in which he subjects himself to continual self-judgment. The passages of the diary hold the salient points of the ideals he strove for in public life and private action. Tarragona, Spain, Museu Nacional Arqueòlogic.

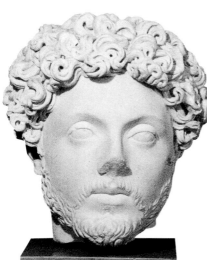

A.D. 96–192

The Antonine Column

The Antonine Column was built in Campus Martius after the death of Marcus Aurelius in order to commemorate his victories along the border on the Danube. It was certainly finished by A.D. 193, when permission was granted to sell the wood from the scaffolding used to build the column.

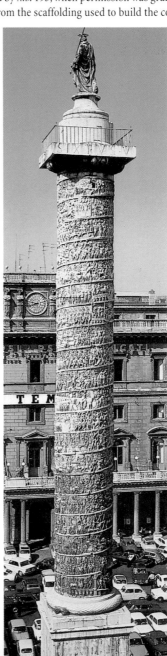

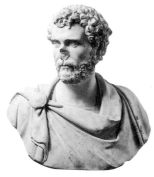

▲ Antoninus Pius, circa A.D. 160. Antoninus Pius is here portrayed with a beard, as Hadrian was, according to a style that would remain until the end of the second century A.D. His expression is intense and human. Perhaps more than in any other preceding time portraits of the emperor resembled those of private citizens. Rome, Museo Palatino.

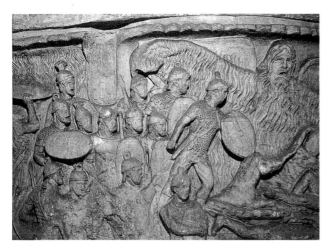

◄ The narrative of the reliefs on the Antonine Column seems weaker than the Trajan Column, and many frames have been inserted simply to fill in the gaps. Certain episodes, however, such as the village fires or the beheadings of barbarian prisoners, have a great, efficient expressiveness.

► A section of the relief. There are 116 scenes on the frieze of the column. A representation of Nike divides them in two series of episodes, which probably refer to military campaigns from A.D. 171 and 173 and 174 and 175. The monument is structured similarly to the Trajan Column, although the spiral-shaped frieze is higher and therefore allows for less-complex development.

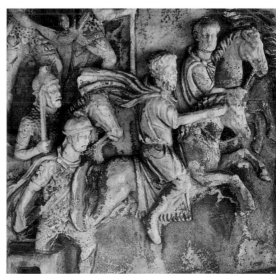

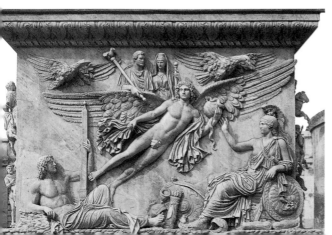

◄ The base of the Column of Antoninus Pius, which features the apotheosis of Antoninus Pius and Faustina. Marcus Aurelius and Lucius Verus built the column in Campus Martius in order to commemorate their adoptive father in the place where his body was cremated. Vatican City, The Vatican Museums.

Marcus Aurelius

This bronze equestrian statue of Marcus Aurelius has survived until today largely because during the Middle Ages it was mistakenly thought to be a statue of Constantine, who was a Christian emperor and therefore respected. Rome, Musei Capitolini.

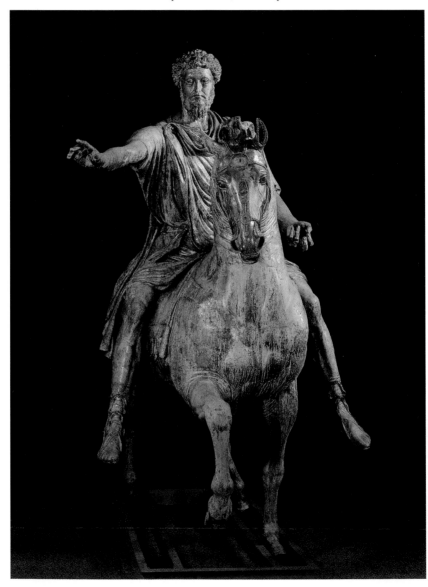

► An Aurelian relief. Dressed in a toga with his head covered, Marcus Aurelius attends the sacrifice of a bull on a temporary altar. The Temple of Jove is visible in the background. This event was definitely connected to the celebration of the triumph over the people of the Danube in a.d. 176. Rome, Palazzo dei Conservatori.

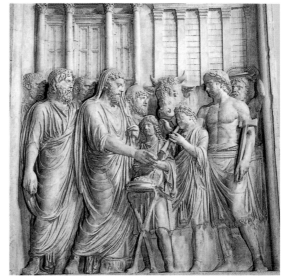

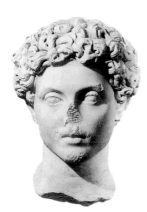

◄ Marcus Aurelius. The future emperor, born in A.D. 121, here is depicted around A.D. 147, when Antoninus Pius brought him to power. Rome, Museo Palatino.

► Faustina the Younger, the daughter of Antoninus Pius and Faustina the Elder, married Marcus Aurelius in A.D. 145. Three years later Lucilla was born from this marriage. She would eventually become the wife of Lucius Verus. Rome, Palazzo Massimo alle Terme.

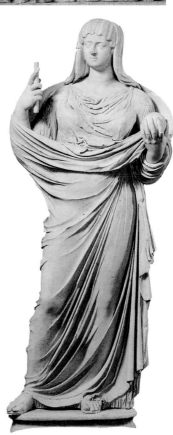

◄ Lucius Verus. This silver bust portrays Marcus Aurelius's adoptive brother, who ruled as co-emperor from A.D. 161 to 169. Part of the loot from a robbery, it was buried near Alexandria around A.D. 250. Turin, Museo di Antichitá.

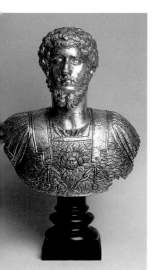

HISTORICAL AND ARTISTIC BACKGROUND

A Turning Point during the Reign of Commodus

Marcus Aurelius had twelve children. Commodus was the only son to survive and was given power at the age of fifteen. Four years later in A.D. 180 he became emperor, putting an end to rulers adopting their successors. The new emperor wasted no time finishing up the wars on the Danube border that his father had left undone. When he returned to Rome he surrounded himself with a court that adored him as they would Hercules and dedicated himself to pleasure and the arena shows he loved. He left power in the hands of a prefect, the head of the imperial guards. This absence of an effective leader at the head of the empire could not last for long, and in A.D. 192 a conspiracy at the palace brought the death of Commodus. Unfortunately a violent economic, social, and moral crisis had already taken hold. The people of the provinces had been occupied with wars on the Danube and in the East for too long, leaving their fields unkempt and their artisan shops empty. The plague had decimated the inhabitants of city and country, and monetary inflation had gone unchecked for the entire second century A.D.

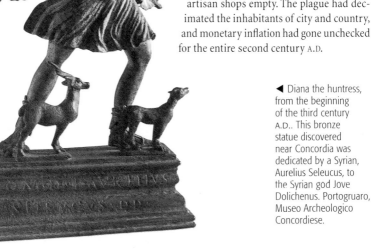

◀ Diana the huntress, from the beginning of the third century A.D.. This bronze statue discovered near Concordia was dedicated by a Syrian, Aurelius Seleucus, to the Syrian god Jove Dolichenus. Portogruaro, Museo Archeologico Concordiese.

▼ Commodus, circa A.D. 190. This bust represents a true political agenda to glorify the prince. The emperor's features are faithfully portrayed, but with attributes typical of Hercules, such as the lion skin on his head, the club, and the apples of Hesperides, the guardians of the tree of the golden apples. Rome, Museo dei Conservatori.

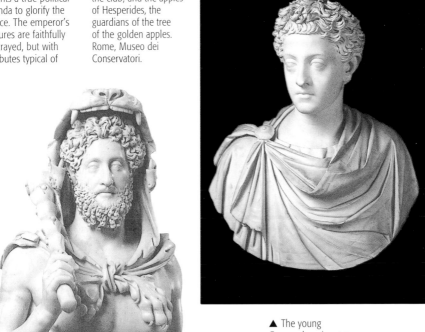

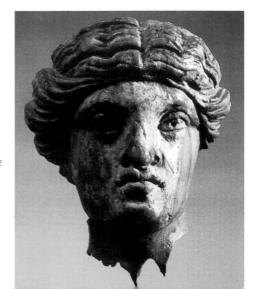

▲ The young Commodus, circa A.D. 176. This was the official bust of the young prince at age fifteen, when he took part in his father's triumph over the people of the Danube. Rome, Musei Capitolini.

▶ A feminine head made of bone from the second or third century A.D. The piece is from a private residence and was recently discovered on Caelian hill. This little head was probably part of the decoration of a wooden piece of furniture, possibly a bed, table, or drawer.

A.D. 96–192

The Portraits of Fayyum

Portraiture in Roman times was very important, but the fragility of the medium meant the loss of almost the whole repertory. Other than some portraits from Pompeii, paintings found in Egypt at the oasis of Fayyum are particularly important. The group is kept in Milan near the Pinacoteca di Brera.

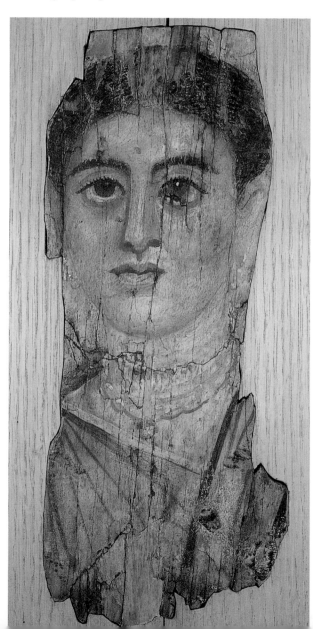

▼ Anubis accompanying the deceased, circa A.D. 175-200. These portraits on wood or cloth were stored in boxes to be eventually applied on mummies. Similar works can be found on linen sheets. Moscow, The Pushkin Museum.

▶ Two brothers, from the second century A.D. This round work of two portraits painted with tempera on wood is very similar to the older painting below of Paquius Proculus and his wife, although the artist's hand seems more supple in this work. Cairo, The Egyptian Museum.

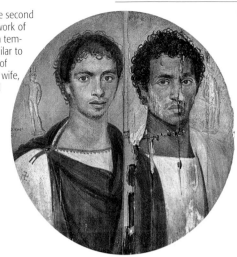

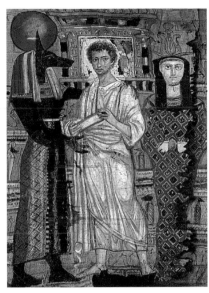

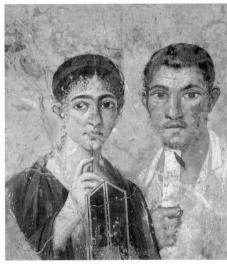

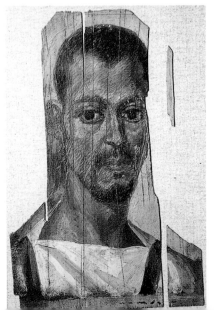

◀ A funeral portrait of a man from the end of the second or the beginning of the third century A.D. The wax painting on wood depicts a character, possibly Greek, who chose to replace an impersonal mask with a true portrait when he was mummified. Paris, Louvre.

▲ A portrait of Paquius Proculus and his wife, circa A.D. 60-70, from Pompeii. His small beard, curly hair, and the papyrus scroll held in his hand indicate that the man is a magistrate, while his wife, who has her hair in the style of the time, poses as a scholarly person. Naples, Museo Archeologico Nazionale.

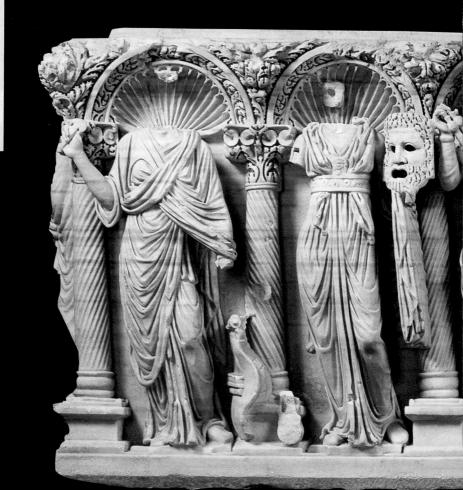

A sarcophagus with statues of the Muses, circa A.D. 270–290. Rome, Palazzo Massimo alle Terme.

Crisis in the Empire:
From the Severans to the Tetrarchy

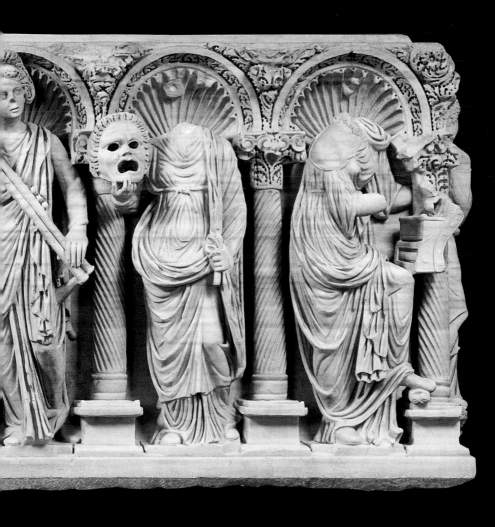

A Turning Point for the Military

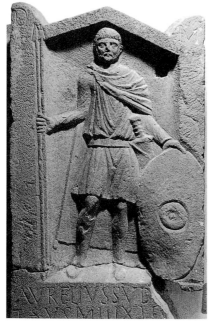

▼ The funeral stele of Aurelius Sudlecentius from the end of the third century A.D. The deceased was a legionnaire from the 11th Claudian Legion, a military unit that was transferred by Trajan to the Danube and then stationed between Pannonia and Moesia. Aquileia, Museo Archeologico Nazionale.

The crisis that began when Commodus was assassinated was not easy to solve. The senatorial aristocracy was not able to present a valid alternative, although it tried to instate an old Roman prefect, Helvius Pertinax, to the throne. The imperial guard deposed him after just three months. Harsh times followed, with almost four years of fighting and civil wars, after which power came to rest steadily in the hands of Septimius Severus. An official of equestrian rank, originally from Africa, he was elected and supported by the military troops of Pannonia. Any links between the new prince and the Roman Senate and Italic traditions were quite scarce, especially since he had married an Eastern woman from a family of priests of the Syrian god Baal. In order to connect himself to the imperial tradition of the second century A.D., he created a fictitious ascendance to the throne. He proclaimed himself the adoptive son of Marcus Aurelius and renamed his son Bassianus after the most prestigious emperor of the preceding dynasty, Marcus Aurelius Antoninus. Bassianus was also known as Caracalla. One of the first items on Septimius Severus's agenda was to reinforce alliances with the troops, who were given economic and juridical privileges.

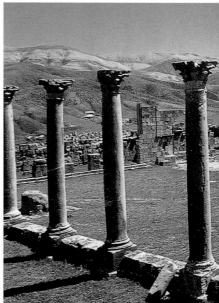

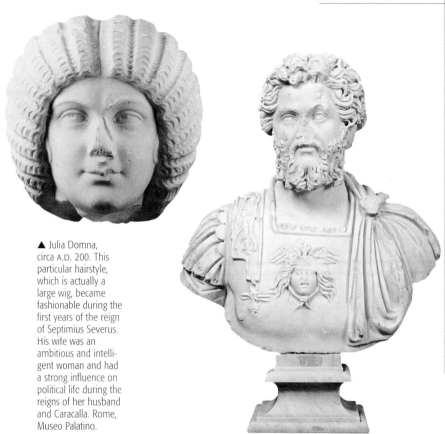

▲ Julia Domna, circa A.D. 200. This particular hairstyle, which is actually a large wig, became fashionable during the first years of the reign of Septimius Severus. His wife was an ambitious and intelligent woman and had a strong influence on political life during the reigns of her husband and Caracalla. Rome, Museo Palatino.

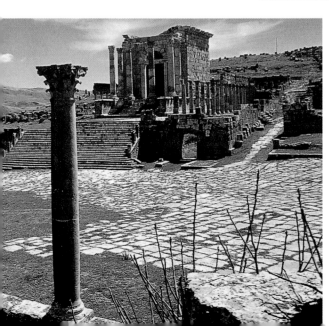

▲ Septimius Severus. This portrait dates to A.D. 196, the year that the new emperor proclaimed himself Marcus Aurelius's son and Commodus's brother. Rome, Palazzo Massimo alle Terme.

◄ Temple of the Severan family, built in the great new forum of the mountain village of Cuicul (present-day Djemila) on the main road that connected Numidia to Mauretania.

Lepcis Magna

Lepcis Magna—in present-day Libya—was already a Roman city in 46 B.C. and was largely developed by Septimius Severus. In fifteen years the emperor transformed it into one of the major African cities, and today its impressive ruins rise from the desert.

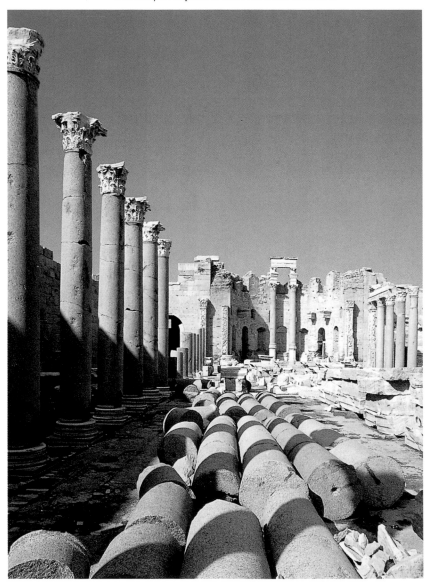

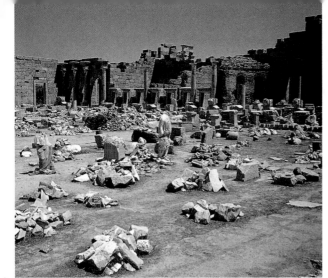

◀ The Roman Forum in Lepcis Magna. The urban restructuring ordered by Septimius Severus provided for the construction of a basilica and an extravagant forum that occupied a hectare of walking area. The new public square was connected to a system of streets and shops.

▼ The Arch of Septimius Severus in Lepcis Magna. Built at the most important crossroads of the main local street, the arch was dedicated to the emperor and his children, Caracalla and Geta. The entire monument was richly decorated.

▶ A sacrificial scene in front of a temple. This is one of the four friezes of the arch honoring Septimius Severus that was built in A.D. 203–204. Two bulls are sacrificed in the presence of the entire imperial family.

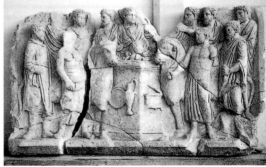

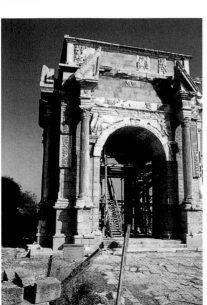

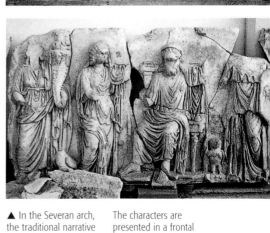

▲ In the Severan arch, the traditional narrative scheme, where figures usually follow one another from left to right, has been changed. The characters are presented in a frontal position and not according to the narrative.

Sculpture in Rome and Africa

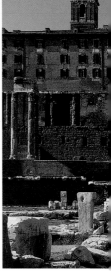

Sculpture in the Severan period is well recorded for Rome and the provinces, especially in Tripolitania and Lepcis Magna, where the emperor was born and a broad urban reconstruction program was put in place. New public buildings were built there along with a new port, and everything was connected to existing neighborhoods by a colonnaded street. Although the ornamentation of the buildings in Lepcis Magna were modeled on Eastern works, they were probably refined by local artisans who had been trained to carve freestanding sculpture for two centuries, thanks to the wealth of rich merchants. In Rome sculptural elements from the previous century prevailed, while at the same time the language of the plebian current in Roman art was added into the mix. For example, the Arch of the Argentari was a monument that signaled a gradual crossover toward the art of late antiquity, especially with its tendency to portray imperial figures disproportionately in a frontal way and out of perspective. A major breakthrough, however, were four great panels that were packed with figures from significant events in the war against the Parthians. They were placed above the side arches of the Arch of Septimius Severus in the Roman Forum, and it would seem that they were modeled after Eastern paintings. The same emperor had sent some large paintings of his exploits from the East along with news of victory, and the Senate exhibited them to the public's admiration.

▲ The Arch of Septimius Severus in Rome. The Senate dedicated it to the emperor in A.D. 203 to celebrate the wars fought against the Parthians. Above the arch was a bronze chariot pulled by six horses surrounded by statues of figures on horseback.

▶ The entranceway to sections of the city the Severans built in Timgad, from the end of the second century A.D. The city of Timgad was founded around A.D. 100 as an official colony for a legion of veterans in a fertile area of present-day Algeria. The area was particularly fortunate during the Severan period.

◀ A relief in Palazzo Sacchetti in Rome. The relief decorated a public building and depicts senators addressing the emperor on the day his children Caracalla and Geta were elected consuls in A.D. 205.

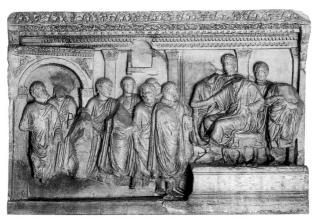

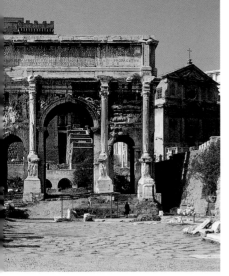

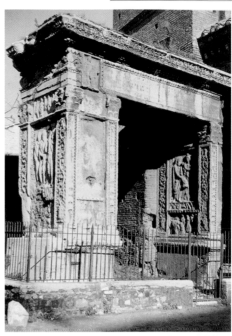

▶ The Arch of the Argentari in Rome. Two rich trade associations, the cattle merchants and moneychangers, built the arch in A.D. 204 in honor of the imperial couple. Here the sixty-year-old Septimius Severus is portrayed with Julia Domna carrying out a sacrifice in the visible internal vault of the arch.

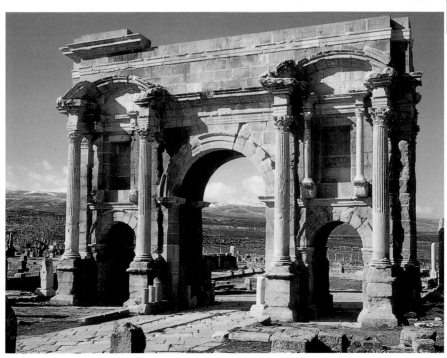

ART AND ARCHITECTURE

Portraits and Sarcophagi

In the third century A.D. portraiture represented some of the most significant works of the time. Individual features with physical characteristics and psychological traits were by now freely fixed in marble and bronze without any residue of Hellenistic schemes. The result was a more complete expression in facial areas, whether the works were official portraits for the imperial family or anonymous. What was also characteristic of this era was the technique of carving short hair or the first signs of a beard with tiny chisel hits. The most credible witness of the artistic currents of the era, however, whether in Rome or the Athenian and Eastern workshops, was a series of monumental sarcophagi. These portrayed symbols and myths that alluded to a resurrection after death. The Eastern faiths, which were quite widespread by now, and Christianity, which was successfully expanding into all social classes, both agreed with this concept of redemption, although with different ideologies. Sarcophagi depicting lion hunts were especially common between A.D. 220 and 270. They were often rendered in compositions that were dense, crowded, and had overlapping figures.

▼ The sarcophagus of Acilia, circa A.D. 270–280. This scene probably represents the procession marking the beginning of a consul's term. On the first of January every year, the court accompanied a newly elected consul to Capitoline hill in order to carry out sacrificial rites. This Greek marble sarcophagus was the work of Eastern teachers and is witness to the high artistic level that private funeral sculptures reached in the third century A.D. Rorne, Palazzo Massimo alle Terme.

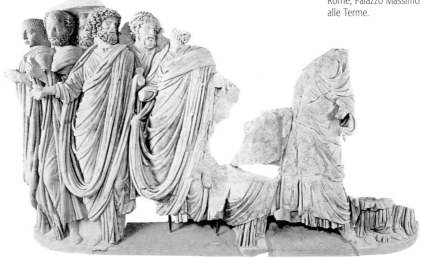

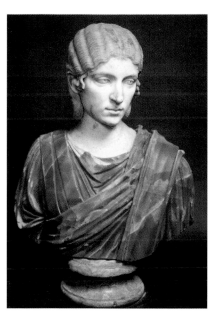

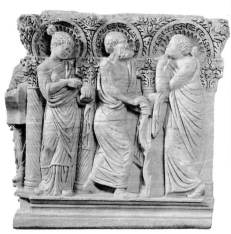

◄ A woman's portrait from the middle of the third century A.D. The bust reflects the era's taste for different types of marble. Her clothing is made of Egyptian alabaster, while her head, with its hair styled in the typical way of the Severan period, is made of white marble. Naples, Museo Archeologico Nazionale.

▼ A sarcophagus with Muses, circa A.D. 270–290. A philosopher in the central niche is flanked by two Muses, an approach that would become quite frequent in funeral reliefs after the middle of the third century A.D. Eastern artists, probably in Rome, made the sarcophagus, since the marble is Italian. Rome, Palazzo Massimo alle Terme.

▼ A sarcophagus with the myth of Ariadne, circa A.D. 235. The face of the sleeping heroine is unfinished because it was probably intended to represent the deceased. The complex scene shows Ariadne left behind in Naxos by Theseus, the hero she fell in love with and gave a ball of thread to so he could find his way out of the Labyrinth after killing the Minotaur. Paris, Louvre.

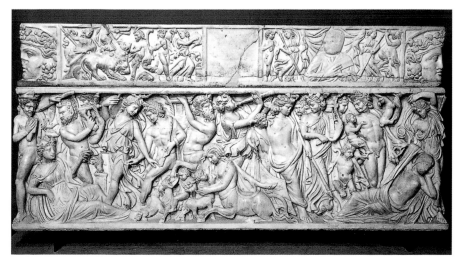

ART AND ARCHITECTURE

The Catacombs

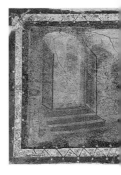

The catacombs began to be developed in Rome and the rest of the empire from the second century A.D. onwards, mostly through private contributions that made land available to dig these cemeteries. This development met the needs of the community of believers, many of whom would not have been able to provide for a dignified burial because of economic problems. These cemeteries were laid out in a deep and intricate web of tunnels where light penetrated through skylights cut out when the catacombs were dug, or through oil lamps. Most of the burial vaults were stacked one on top of another and closed with marble slabs, tiles, or tufa blocks that were sealed with lime and sometimes inscribed with the name of the deceased. Areas near the tombs of martyrs were especially developed in some cemeteries so followers could be buried nearby. These holy places continued to be frequented even during the fifth century A.D., when catacomb burials were discontinued. Only in the modern age were these cemeteries erroneously thought to be refuges for believers during persecutions against Christians, which were not very many and occurred during the second half of the third century A.D.

◀ The Good Shepherd Cubicle, from the end of the second or the beginning of the third century A.D. The delicate geometric motif on a cream background is useful in articulating the decorated surfaces in a regular order. Rome, The Catacombs of Domitilla.

▼ The catacombs of Saints Peter and Marcellus in Rome, circa A.D. 310–330. The panels are decorated with various scenes from the Old Testament, such as Daniel in the lion's den and Moses making water flow from the rock.

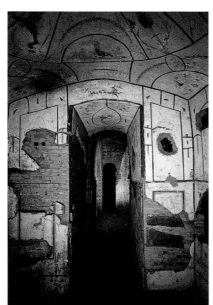

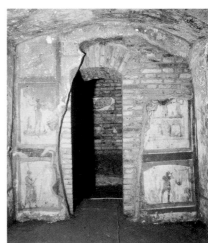

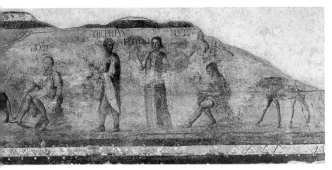

◄ Orpheus and Euridice, from a third century A.D. burial vault in Ostia. These vaults were burial chambers destined for large families and groups with recesses for urns of ashes. One vault contained the remains of more than three thousand servants and freemen from Livia or other associations. Vatican City, The Vatican Museum.

▶ Samson fights the Philistines, from the middle of the fourth century A.D. Here the great central figure, fortified with spiritual power, battles the Philistines with only the jawbone of an ass. Rome, The Catacombs of Via Compagni.

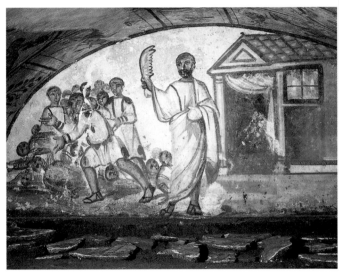

▼ A lunette with a banquet scene. Certain episodes of the Holy Scriptures were given symbolic value. Adam and Eve recalled original sin, and a banquet was a memory of the sacrament of the Eucharist.

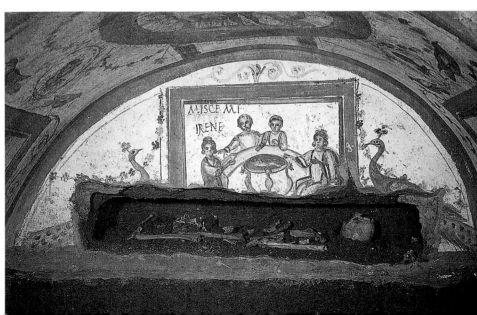

The Baths of Caracalla

The imposing ruins of the Baths of Caracalla dominate a vast area on the slopes of Aventino hill. They were built between A.D. 212 and 217, restored numerous times, and stopped working in A.D. 537 when Vitigus, the Ostragoth king, cut off the aqueduct.

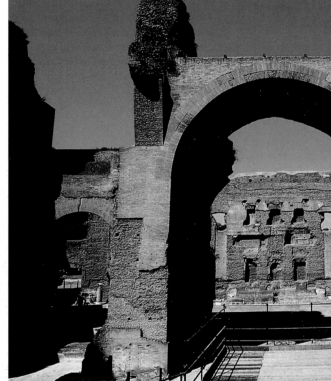

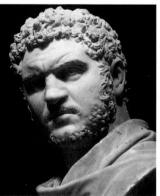

▲ Caracalla. Septimius Severus had chosen his sons, Caracalla and Geta, to succeed him, but at his death their relationship became more and more tense until Caracalla had his brother assassinated in A.D. 212. He remained supreme sovereign until he himself was killed in A.D. 217. Naples, Museo Archeologico Nazionale.

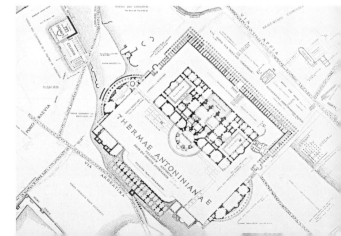

▼ This granite bathtub at the Piazza Farnese in Rome was excavated in the sixteenth century from the Baths of Caracalla, together with another that sits in the same square. Numerous works of art that must have decorated the thermal bath area were also discovered. Among these were three enormous Farnese sculptures now at the Museo Archeologico Nazionale in Naples.

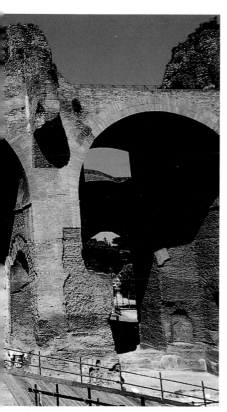

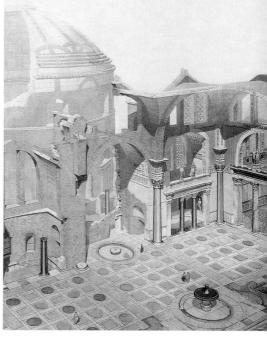

◄ Inside the Baths of Caracalla the process of taking a bath was perfectly identical in the two halves of the unheated building. The two areas had some rooms in common, such as heated rooms, a basilica, and a pool.

► The *frigidarium*, in a nineteenth-century reconstruction by Eugéne Violet-le-Duc. This unheated environment was usually richly decorated. It was among the final steps of the bathing process in the thermal building, which began with the gym and the Turkish bath (*laconicum*).

Invasions and Disorder

▼ Gallienus. The son of Valerian, Gallienus became a partner in power with his father in A.D. 253. After Valerian was humiliatingly captured in A.D. 260 Gallienus was left alone to guide the empire. He did nothing—and probably could do nothing—to free his father from a Persian prison. Rome, Palazzo Massimo alle Terme.

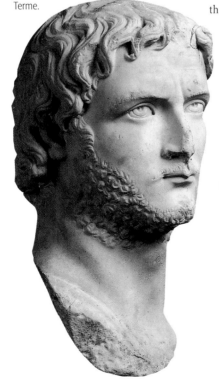

Elagabalus and Alexander Severus, the last two rulers of the Severan family, were both too young and inexperienced. They were placed in the imperial succession largely because of the women of the ruling family, Julia Maesa and Julia Mamea. In A.D. 235, however, even Alexander and his mother were assassinated. A period of anarchy followed in Rome, destined to last more than forty years. Many emperor-soldier figures came close to guiding the empire, although they were never able to establish a decisive central authority that balanced the ever-increasing power of the military. The strong ability of the army to protect the borders of the empire made it, in effect, the situation's true sovereign. The emperors of this time were hardly able to oversee political and economic administration due to the fact that they were constantly engaged in defending the borders of the empire. One of the crucial points of the empire's defense was the Balkan region, so much so that the empire's political center eventually moved toward that area. In A.D. 268 Claudius the Goth—the first emperor of Illyrian origin—ascended to the throne. Perhaps the most illustrious example of the Illyrian emperors who followed him was Diocletian.

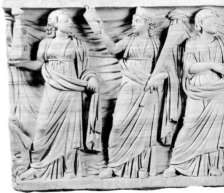

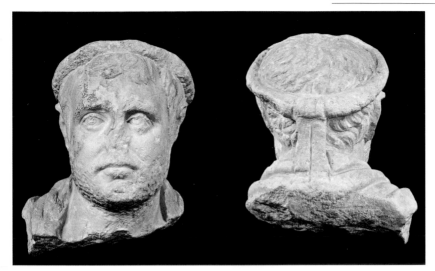

▲ Balbinus, A.D. 238. This emperor was a general in his sixties when he ascended to the throne and was killed after just ninety days. This portrait has his head circled by a laurel crown with a ribbon that falls to his shoulders. The sculpture is probably from a Greek workshop. Rome, Palazzo Massimo alle Terme.

▼ The Sarcophagus of Annona, circa A.D. 270–280. The deceased, who could have been a prefect in Annona who oversaw the importation and distribution of grain, is here depicted in the center of the relief holding his wife's hand. Her hairstyle is the same as the fashion of Ulpia Severina (A.D. 270–275), the wife of Aurelian. Rome, Palazzo Massimo alle Terme.

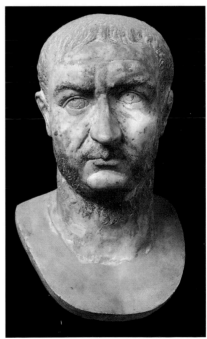

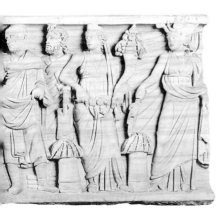

▲ Valerian. This emperor had already been in power for seven years when he was captured in A.D. 260 in Edessa, in northern Mesopotamia, during an attempt to check the new Persian state of Shapur the 1st. Rome, Musei Capitolini.

Rome as Fortress: The Aurelian Walls

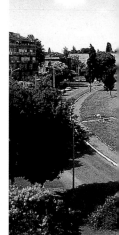

By the end of the republican period the old series of walls that surrounded Rome had lost their initial function, and the borders of the inhabited areas remained the ancient *pomerium*, the city limits set for religious and administrative purposes that were enlarged various times in the course of the centuries. Nevertheless, the need for new walls became apparent during the extremely severe economic and political crisis of the third century A.D. Germanic tribes had already laid siege to Aquileia during the reign of Marcus Aurelius, but it would be a century later before it seemed that enemies would threaten Rome. Emperor Aurelian, who was constantly involved in wars that were always further and further away, decided to give the city a new group of walls. Begun in A.D. 271, they were quickly finished in less than ten years. In the beginning these walls were a modest defense for the city, although they were enough to stop armies who were not able to besiege Rome for a long period. The walls were eventually reinforced several times, with the most important work done during the reign of Acadius and Honorius in A.D. 401–402. The fortification is almost nineteen kilometers long, and various buildings are encompassed within the perimeter, such as the Castrense amphitheater. The walls were completed in a rush.

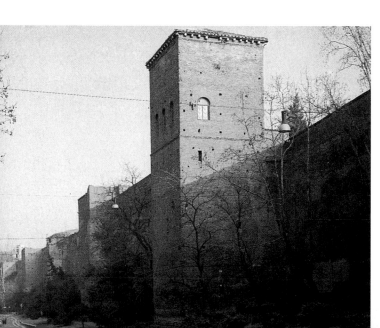

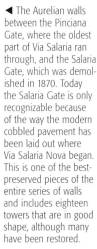

◀ The Aurelian walls between the Pinciana Gate, where the oldest part of Via Salaria ran through, and the Salaria Gate, which was demolished in 1870. Today the Salaria Gate is only recognizable because of the way the modern cobbled pavement has been laid out where Via Salaria Nova began. This is one of the best-preserved pieces of the entire series of walls and includes eighteen towers that are in good shape, although many have been restored.

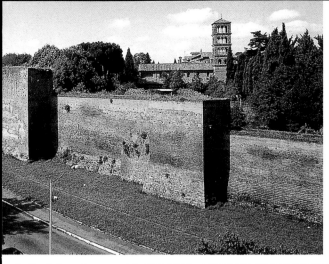

◀ The Aurelian wall on Viale Metronio between Metronio Gate and Latina Gate, where the street of the latter name crossed. The travertine façade dates to the construction ordered by Aurelian. It was hardly changed during reconstruction by Honorius.

▶ The Ostiense Gate (or Porta San Paolo), together with the San Sebastiano Gate, are definitely the best preserved. A variety of alterations can be seen. This is where Via Ostiense began, which connected Rome with its port, Ostia. Totila's Goths entered the city through this gate in A.D. 594.

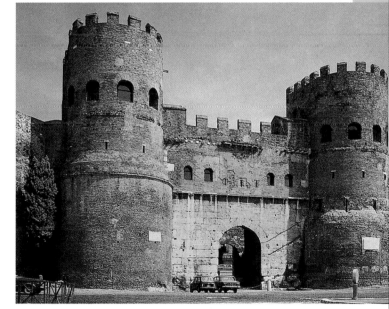

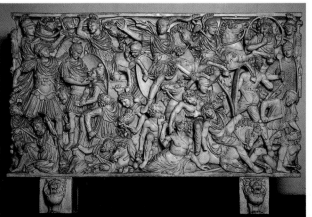

◀ The Great Ludovisi Sarcophagus, circa A.D. 250. Three levels depict the action: the victors are shown on the highest level, those fighting occupy the second, and the fallen victims of war are on the third. The general on horseback with a cross on his forehead has been identified as Hostilian, the son of Emperor Decius. Rome, Palazzo Altemps.

The Tetrarchy: Toward a New Peace

Gaius Valerius Diocles was born in Dalmatia and made his career in the army by becoming head of Emperor Numerian's imperial guard. After the emperor died at the hands of his father-in-law Aper, who was praetorian prefect, Diocles was entrusted with executing the death sentence of the assassin. Afterwards he was immediately proclaimed emperor by the troops and entered triumphantly into Nicomedia in Bithynia on November 17, A.D. 284. Power was once again solidly in the hands of one man. The new sovereign wanted to resurrect the traditional image and prestige of the emperor but immediately realized that in order to reach his goal of moral, political, and military renewal, he had to prepare to deeply reform the empire on an institutional level. With the intention of unifying the empire culturally, he imposed the use of Latin in all the provinces and even Latinized his own name from Diocles to Diocletian. At the same time, however, he stripped Rome of its capital role and moved his residence to Nicomedia. He also reinforced the divine image of the emperor, founding an absolute power akin to a theocracy. This was based on careful management of the sovereign's public image and a rigid ceremonial court.

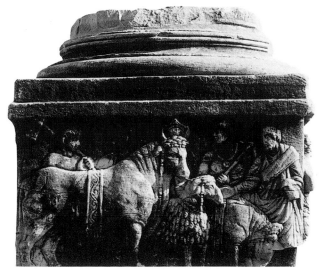

◀ A *decennali* base from the Roman Forum, A.D. 303. This was a base from an honorary column built to celebrate the tenth year of a Caesar's reign. On the west side of the base a relief depicts the sacrifice of a bull, a sheep, and a pig, to seek the gods' favor (*suovetaurilia*).

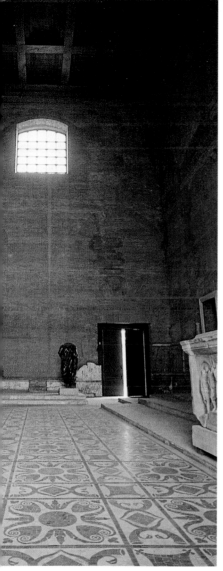

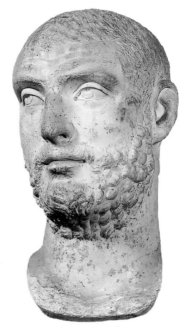

▲ Carinus (A.D. 283–285) succeeded his father, Carus, as ruler of the western empire. His brother Numerian governed the eastern part. He defeated Diocletian twice in the same year, only to be killed by his troops, leaving the empire in the hands of his opponent. Rome, Musei Capitolini.

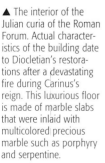

▲ The interior of the Julian curia of the Roman Forum. Actual characteristics of the building date to Diocletian's restorations after a devastating fire during Carinus's reign. This luxurious floor is made of marble slabs that were inlaid with multicolored precious marble such as porphyry and serpentine.

▶ A red porphyry column with two tetrarchs, from the beginning of the fourth century A.D. This pair, together with other similar examples, like the more famous one at San Marco in Venice, constitutes a true break with the artistic canons of antiquity. Vatican City, Biblioteca Apostolica Vaticana.

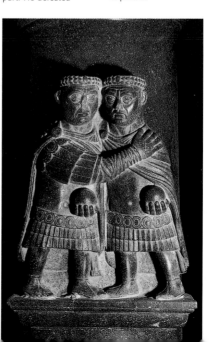

The Baths of Diocletian

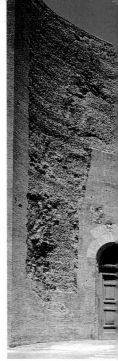

During the entire imperial era, numerous public thermal baths had emerged in Rome. In order to satisfy the public, they were continually increasing in size. A bath, depending on a person's physical conditions or social status, could be either a simple hygienic need or a refined pleasure. Even the higher classes frequently went to the immense public baths despite having a small version (*balneum*) at home. The Baths of Diocletian was the largest bathing system ever built in the city, serving the densely populated neighborhoods on the edges of Quirinal, Viminal, and Esquiline hills. It was built between A.D. 298–306 by demolishing several older buildings from a previous era, as factory stamps on bricks attest. The use of stamps had disappeared during the course of the third century A.D. but evidently resurfaced for this particular construction. The dimensions of the system were so large that they allowed more than three thousand people to use it at the same time. This doubled the already impressive baths of Caracalla. Probably in order to serve a less-popular area, Constantine had a new thermal bath system installed in the same neighborhood a decade later. Thus in the middle of the fourth century A.D. the population of Rome—almost a million and a half people—could count on there being almost nine-hundred *balnea* and eleven large establishments.

▲ The Basilica of Santa Maria degli Angeli was built within the Baths of Diocletian, and its façade is made up of one of the apses of the areas where hot baths were taken (*calidarium*). Most of the *calidarium* has by now disappeared.

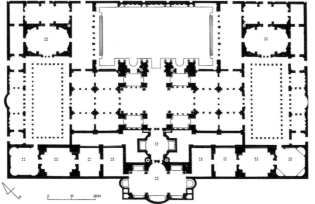

◄ The Baths of Diocletian take up an area of almost 380 by 370 meters. On the northeastern side there was a large trapezoidal cistern called the *botte di Termini*. It was more than ninety meters long and fed by a branch of the Aqua Marcia aqueduct. Memory of the thermal baths remains in the name of today's Roma Termini train station.

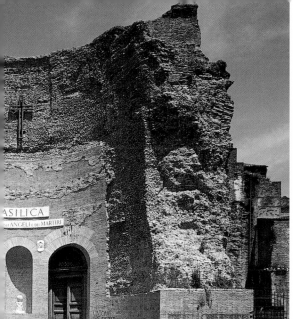

▼ A great octagonal hall with semicircular niches occupies the northwest corner of the building, which is now an exhibition hall at the Museo alle Terme. The room has long been used as a planetarium and was recently restored.

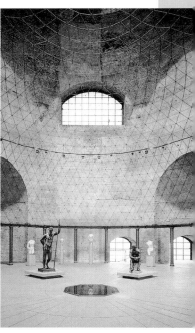

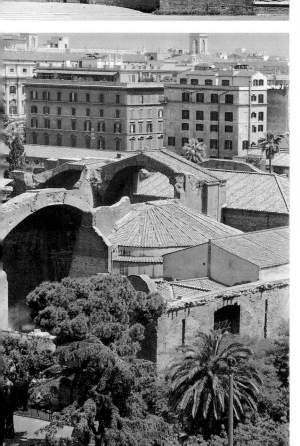

◄ The best-preserved structures are those of the central complex, though there are still recognizable traces of the large surrounding wall. Those areas that have been incorporated within later buildings have survived particularly well.

Diocletian's Reforms

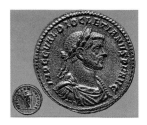

$\mathbf{M}$oving the capital to Nicomedia had profound repercussions. It made it clear that it was impossible to govern the military and political situation from Rome, and the new imperial residence allowed for the control of the borders along the Danube and to the east. Moving the capital east was balanced by partnering one of Diocletian's brothers-in-arms to the throne. Maximian was charged with the western sector of the empire. In A.D. 293 this dual government was transformed into a tetrarchy when two Caesars, Galerius and Constantius Chlorus, were joined to the throne, marked in succession according to the old principle of merit. Besides committing himself to maintaining the eastern front, Diocletian also instated a vast program of reforms. A half million strong, the army was reinforced and reorganized after almost a half century of anarchy. Restrengthening the hierarchy of functionaries, who would become a kind of social caste, reformed government administration. Diocletian also began a radical restructuring of the provinces, which had increased in number. They were grouped into dioceses, which in turn were united under a prefecture. For the first time Italy found itself on the same level as other imperial provinces because of this reorganization.

▼ Having left power in A.D. 305, Diocletian built an enormous fortified villa in his native land of Dalmatia. He spent the last years of his life there. The building was conceptualized as a military camp surrounded by a towered wall.

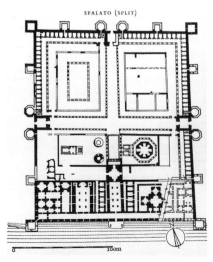

SPALATO (SPLIT)

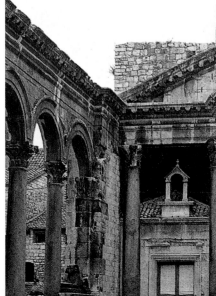

◀ A gold coin of Diocletian dating from before the reforms of A.D. 286–287. The reverse side holds the figure of Jove with a lightning bolt, along with the legend. Aquileia, Museo Archeologico Nazionale.

▼ Robert Adam's 1754 depiction of Diocletian's villa. The villa foreshadowed architectural solutions that would be reused for building medieval castles and monasteries.

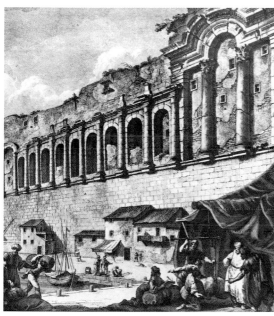

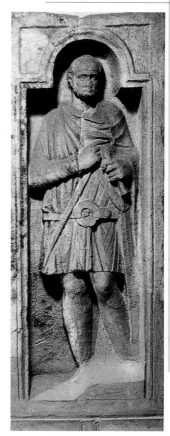

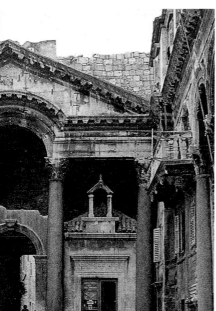

◀ A peristyle from Diocletian's palace in Split, Croatia. The residence, which modern-day Split was built around, had one side that faced directly onto the sea, where the entrance was. Inside residential quarters gave the villa the luxurious look of an imperial residence.

▲ A funeral stele of a centurion from the end of the third century A.D. In this tall, rectangular stele the internal frame with a Pannonian-type arch and the presentation of the figure in its entirety follow models that were popular in provincial areas of Central Europe. The face of the statue seems to have barbaric traits. Aquileia, Museo Archeologico Nazionale.

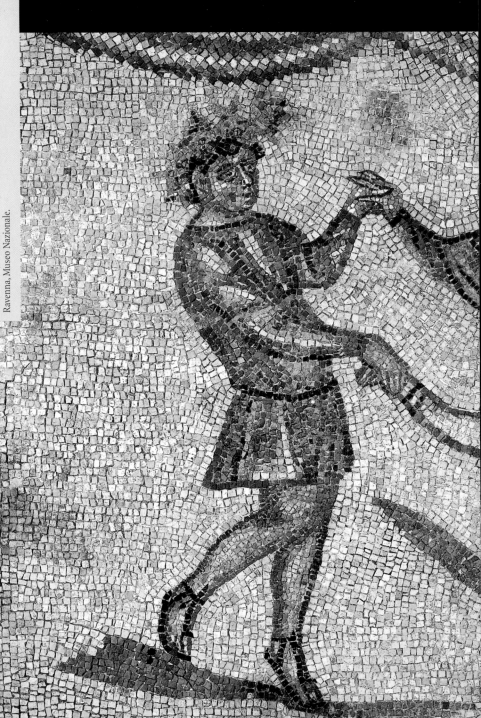

The Dance of the Seasons, from the middle of the fourth century A.D. Ravenna, Museo Nazionale.

The Fall of the Empire:
Epilogue to an Ancient World

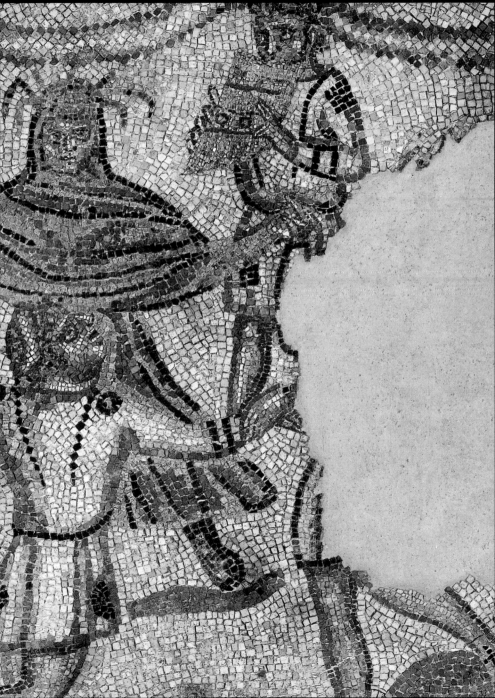

The Christian Empire

▼ A figure in a toga from the first half of the second century A.D. This head, which was sculpted later than the rest of the body, has been hypothetically reconstructed as the portrait of Constantius Gallus. He was Julian the Apostate's brother, Constantine's nephew, and ruler of the eastern empire between A.D. 351 and 354. In that year he was decapitated by order of Constantius the 2nd because of his cruelty. Rome, Palazzo Massimo alle Terme.

I n A.D. 305 Diocletian and Maximian abdicated the throne, leaving power in the hands of their chosen heirs: Galerius in the east and Constans in the west. The latter died the following year, and the military proclaimed his son Constantine as emperor while the Roman people elected Maxentius, Maximian's son. Dramatic years followed, when various Caesars and emperors were eliminated. Finally only Maxentius and Constantine were left in the contest to control the western empire, and Constantine was victorious near Milvio Bridge in Rome in A.D. 312. He was also eventually able to oust Emperor Licinius of the eastern empire in A.D. 324, thereby reuniting the Roman Empire. In A.D. 313 Constantine had pronounced an edict in Milan legitimizing all religions, overturning the religious politics of Diocletian. The intermingling of church and state affairs continued, especially after the authorities recognized church courts and their rulings in civil cases and when the emperor intervened in disputes that hounded the Church. In A.D. 325 the first ecumenical council was convened in Nicea in order to condemn the Arian heresy.

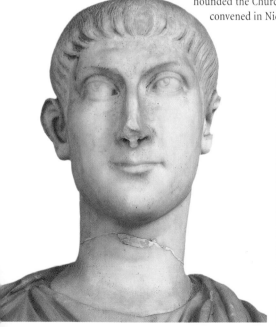

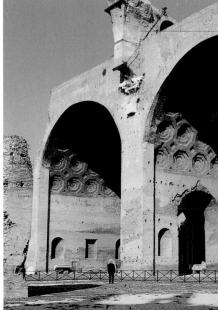

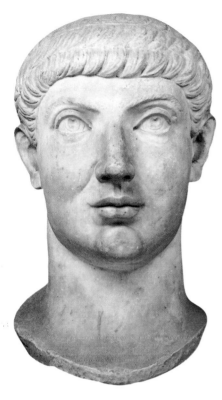

◄ A colossal head, this sculpture portrays one of Constantine's sons: either Constantius the 2nd, who was the third son of the emperor and held the throne in the east from A.D. 337 to 361, or Constans, a fourth or fifth son of the emperor. He ruled the western empire between A.D. 337 and 350, until he was dethroned and killed in Gaul by Magnentius. Rome, Palazzo dei Conservatori.

▼ A knight of Altino, circa A.D. 310–325. This tiny bronze statue has been identified as a portrait of Constantine on horseback. Its principal traits are the radiating crown, attributed to the sun worship that the emperor definitively overthrew in A.D. 324, and a beardless face. No ruler since Trajan had had a beard. Vienna, Kunsthistorisches Museum.

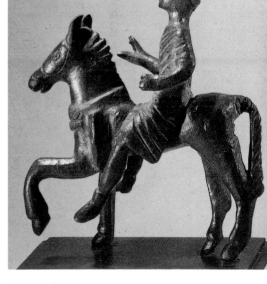

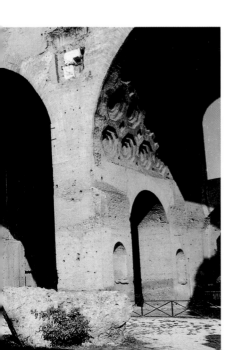

◄ The Basilica of Maxentius in the Roman Forum. The construction of this enormous building was the work of Maxentius, though it was soon modified by Constantine and then restructured once more toward the end of the fourth century A.D.

The Arch of Constantine

This honorary arch, the largest of its kind to survive, was situated along the road where triumphal parades passed toward the Temple of Jove on Capitoline hill. It celebrates Constantine's victory over Maxentius in the Battle of Milvio Bridge and the ten-year anniversary of his reign in A.D. 315.

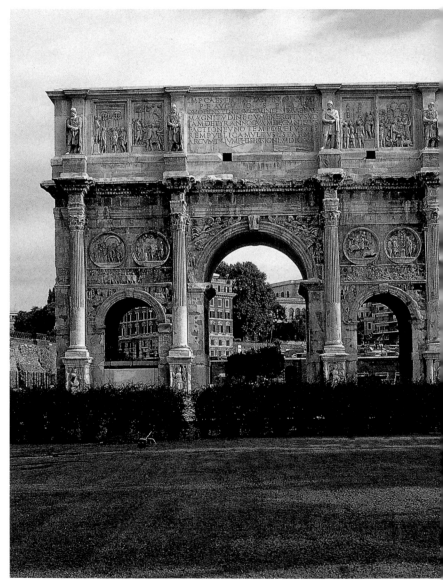

▶ A Dacian prisoner, circa A.D. 107–113. Besides the eight *pavonazzetto* marble statues of prisoners, the arch also includes a huge frieze from the age of Trajan divided in four panels and placed on the short ends of the monument and in the interior of the central arch. The frieze was originally made to decorate the attic of the Ulpia Basilica in the Trajan Forum.

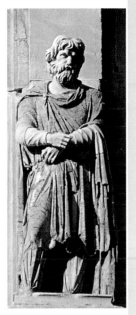

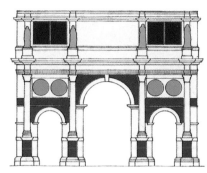

▲ The arch is decorated by marble slabs with reliefs. Many were originally taken from other monuments of earlier eras. Statues from the time of Trajan are in yellow, round reliefs from Hadrian's rule are in blue, reliefs from the reign of Marcus Aurelius are in red, and original decorations from Constantine's reign are in brown.

▼ A scene of sacrifice in a military camp, circa A.D. 175–180. The Aurelian reliefs depict scenes of military campaigns that Marcus Aurelius waged against Germanic tribes. They were originally created for an arch on the slopes of Capitoline hill that celebrated the victories and triumph of the emperor.

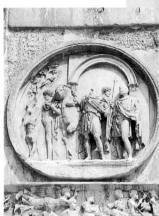

▲ *Above*, a hunting party departs, circa A.D. 130–134. Reliefs from Hadrian's rule perhaps once decorated a temple dedicated to Antinous. *Below*, a section of the historical frieze from the era of Constantine that narrates the warlike exploits of the emperor as well as peacetime events.

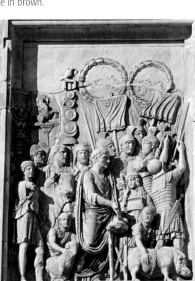

Treveri

Augusta Treverorum had already been founded in the Augustan period and soon became the principal city in northeast Gaul. It was an important commercial center of trade with the Rhine basin and was the seat of the procurator for the provinces of Belgica and the two Germanys. Toward the end of the second century A.D. a wall was built around it with a large northern entrance, known today as Porta Nigra. It became the residence for the emperor of the western empire beginning with Maximian and Constantius Chlorus and became the capital of the prefecture of Gaul in A.D. 297. At the beginning of the fifth century A.D. the city was abandoned to the raiding Franks.

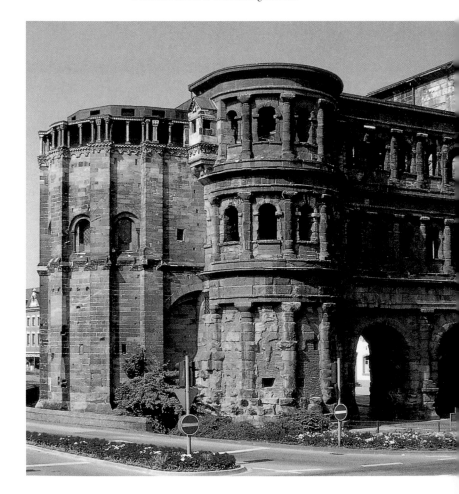

▶ The Palatine Hall in Treveri, circa A.D. 310. Built on a preexisting structure, this basilica was perhaps the seat of the imperial procurator. It is an immense, rectangular hall with an apse measuring fifty-eight meters long by twenty-nine meters wide (in Roman feet this was two hundred by a hundred). Two series of large windows provide for interior lighting, and today the building is still extremely well preserved.

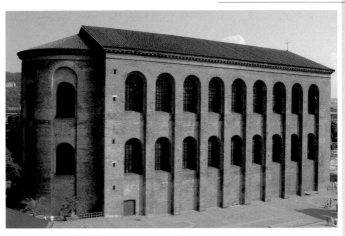

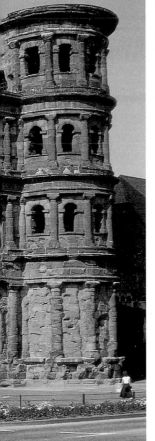

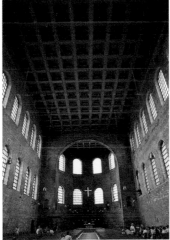

◀ The interior of the Palatine Hall in Treveri. The floor of the hall is of colored marble and was heated by a hot air system similar to those used in thermal baths.

▼ The imperial thermal baths in Treveri. This building was begun by Constantine and finished by Valentinian the 1st circa A.D. 370. The architecture, with its Eastern influence, demonstrates the high level of skill that architects achieved in the new capital.

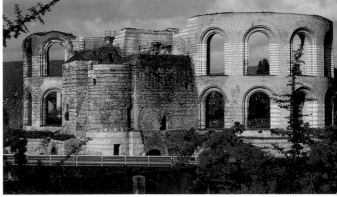

Marble Inlay and Mosaics

In the fourth century A.D. it became fashionable to decorate luxurious rooms with colored marble tiles instead of paintings using a technique called *opus sectile* (a work achieved with cut marble). The first examples of this technique, probably developed in Egypt, go back to the age of Claudius. Panels were most likely sent from the Egyptian workshops ready for wall installation. Especially refined examples of this inlay work, executed in colored marble, precious stones, glass, and mother-of-pearl, can be found in panels from wall facings of a hall built by Junius Basso, a consul in A.D. 331. Important innovations occurred for floor mosaics. The provinces of Africa, Byzancena, Numidia, and Mauretania (present-day Tunisia, Algeria, and Morocco) developed an artistic culture that was for the most part autonomous and had a unique repertory. Besides the usual mythological portrayals, artists from these provinces preferred themes from real life, especially hunting and farming scenes. These were carried out with an extremely intense sense of color, expressed with local marbles and glass.

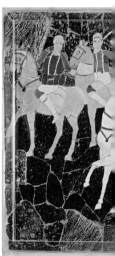

▼ An *opus sectile* panel from the first half of the fourth century A.D. from the Basilica of Junius Basso. A two-horse chariot is driven by a consul (could this be Junius Basso?) and is followed by four horsemen who belong to the four different factions of the circus as illustrated by their different colored costumes. Rome, Palazzo Massimo alle Terme.

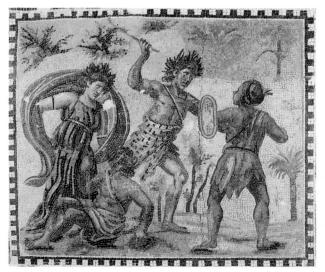

◄ A mosaic depicting a fight between Dionysos and Indians from the first half of the fourth century A.D. Greek literature told of Dionysos's expeditions to the East. These extended as far as India. Rome, Palazzo Massimo alle Terme.

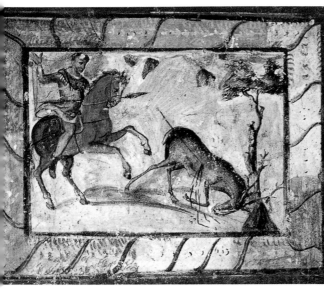

◄ A hunting scene from the fourth century A.D. Hunting on foot or horseback—with or without dogs—was one of the main entertainments for people in areas such as Spain, where wild animals were in abundance. Images of the hunt in floor decorations, modeled after African scenes, also became exaltations of the virility and virtuous education of a rich owner. Merida, Spain, Museo Nacional de Arte Romano.

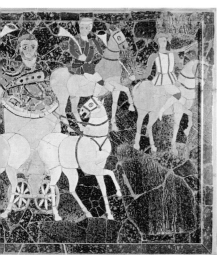

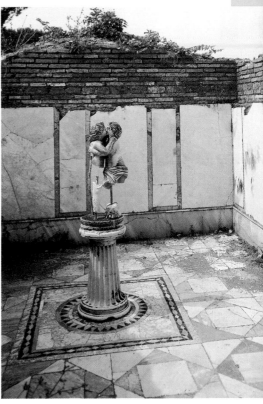

► The House of Eros and Psyche in Ostia, from the third century A.D. Ostia had been the main port for Rome since the first century A.D. and was the center for officials and weapons guilds. At the beginning of the first century A.D. merchants who arrived at the port were mostly from Italy, but during the second century, imports from Africa, Spain, and Gaul became more intensified after an economic crisis hit Italy and the economies of the provinces emerged.

MASTERPIECES OF ART

Piazza Armerina

The Casale Villa was a luxurious residence in Sicily that dated from the beginning of the fourth century A.D. in Piazza Armerina. Extensive mosaic floors are preserved there. They were partially the work of African artisans and included the mosaic *The Great Hunt* (see below).

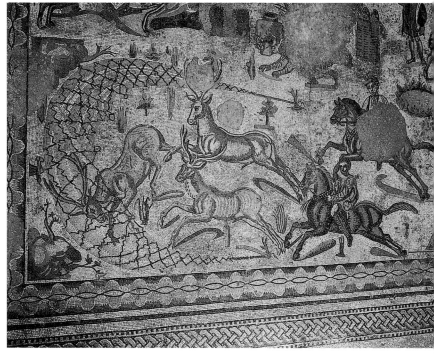

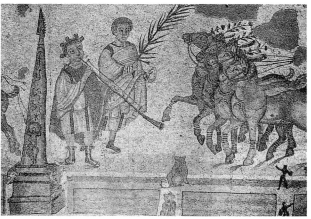

◄ The winning chariot finishes on the racetrack at the Circus Maximus in Rome. This is a detail from the mosaic floor of a hall with two apses in the thermal complex of the Casale Villa. *At left*, a trumpeter with a red, fringed cape and another celebrity in a toga are offering palms to the winner.

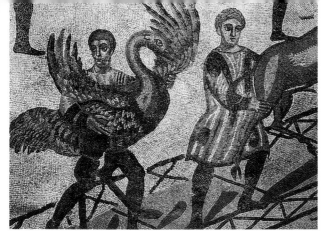

◄ Transporting live animals from Africa was no simple maneuver, especially when the animals had to be lured into wooden cages with sliding doors using live bait such as antelopes or gazelles. In this case, however, ostriches are simply picked up and brought aboard the ship.

► In the receiving hall of the Casale Villa a mosaic telling how animals that were destined for the amphitheater shows were hunted takes up a space of nearly three hundred square meters. The story is set in all the known world of the time, as suggested by the many details of countries. Here, armed men are capturing a wild boar in a forest, aided by a pack of hunting dogs.

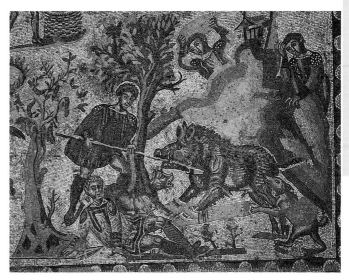

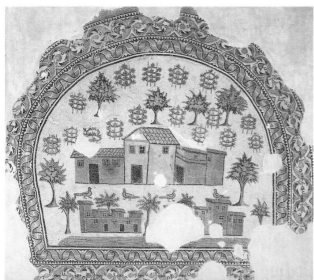

◄ A mosaic of a country villa. In African floor mosaics life in the large properties was often illustrated, including annexed houses of the colonists, fields, ceramic factories, and animals, almost to the point that they resemble land registry drawings. Tunisia, Museo del Bardo.

The Mausoleum of Constantina

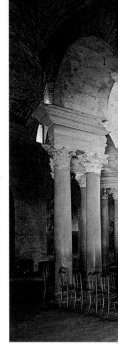

Built on Via Nomentana for one of Constantine's daughters, Constantina, just before her death in A.D. 354, this mausoleum was extremely innovative in terms of architecture. The large, circular construction—today the Basilica di Santa Costanza, laterally connected to the Basilica di Sant'Agnese—is made up of a barrel-vaulted corridor ring, at the center of which is an elevated drum raised by twelve pairs of columns and covered by a dome. The sarcophagus destined to hold the remains of Constantina was originally placed in one of the niches in the wall. The vault of the annular corridor features a mosaic with a white background. It was achieved using the same technique and care that the floors were and confirms that the vault and floor decorations were made to match. The wall mosaics and those of the cupola have largely disappeared, but their general theme can be reconstructed from the foundations discovered behind later designs from the Renaissance. Biblical scenes with miniature figures were above running water with cherubs and fish, a sign that Christian iconography still occupied a reduced space in this Constantinian-era construction.

◀ The mosaic vault of the annual corridor. Many geometric motifs appear in this detail, as do Bacchic motifs, which are the prevalent symbolic theme here. Rome, Mausoleo di Costantina.

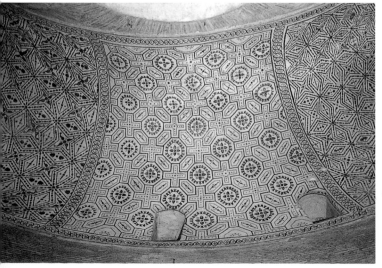

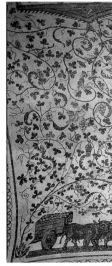

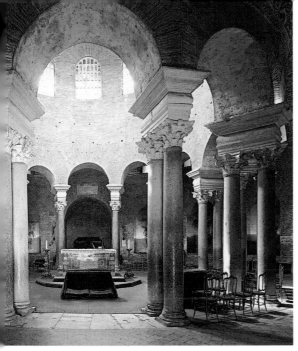

◀ The Mausoleum of Constantina, which today is the Church of Santa Costanza. Some of the building's decorations led it to be called the Temple of Bacchus during the Renaissance. There are porphyry harvesters on the sarcophagus that appear throughout the interior and Bacchic motifs that run through the vault. There was another rotunda that Constantine had ordered built at the doors of Rome as a mausoleum for his mother, Helena, who was proclaimed a saint; its ruins are known today as Tor Pignattara.

▼ The mosaic vault of the corridor ring. Rome, Mausoleo di Costantina. A similar mosaic to this one is part of a Christian mausoleum from fourth-century Spain. It was perhaps destined for Constans, Constantine's youngest son, who was assassinated in the Pyrenees in A.D. 350.

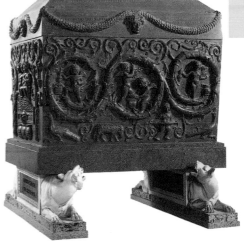

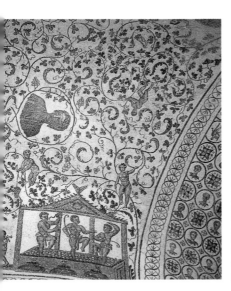

▲ The sarcophagus of Constantina, circa A.D. 340. The sarcophagus is made of red porphyry and was modeled after that of Saint Helena, Constantine's mother, which was also of red porphyry. Both were surely made in the East. The decorative motif of cherubs and vines was commonly found on sarcophagi and catacombs and matches the mosaic panels of the corridor ring. Vatican City, The Vatican Museum.

Aquileia

Founded in 181 B.C., Aquileia soon became the quickest developing city in northern Italy and an important commercial center thanks to craftsmanship and, above all, its port. The city hosted the imperial residence under Diocletian and Constantine and was a church diocese as early as the fourth century A.D. After Attila conquered it in A.D. 452, its inhabitants moved to new urban centers, along with other groups from inland cities. From Grado to Caorle, Torcello, and Chioggia, all these peoples laid the groundwork for what was to become Venice. In the southern side of the Teodoro Hall (see below) an entire floor mosaic of 750 square meters has survived with borders of garlands, animals, and birds all arranged geometrically.

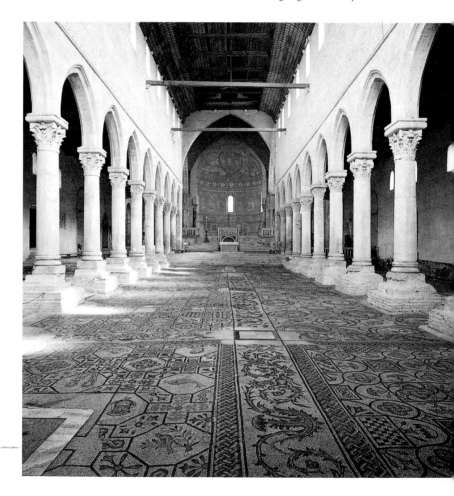

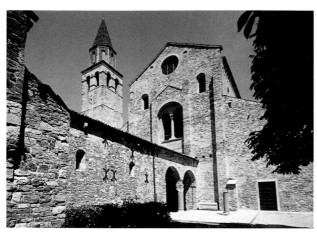

◀ The façade of the basilica in Aquileia. This building's reconstruction, over what was probably a preexistent Roman house, goes back to the beginning of the fourth century A.D. and possibly some years before the building of the Roman basilicas in honor of Peter and Paul in A.D. 322. It was set in motion by Theodorus, who was the first bishop elected after the liberalization of all professed religions in the empire.

▼ The sepulchral monument of the Cunii family in Aquileia from the end of the first century B.C. The sepulcher and spire were derived from Hellenistic and Eastern models. At its center is a statue of the deceased.

▶ Jonah and the sea monster, from a mosaic in the southern side of the Teodoro Hall. Jonah is spit onto a raft by a sea monster in a sea rich with fish. In the next scene he rests under a plant.

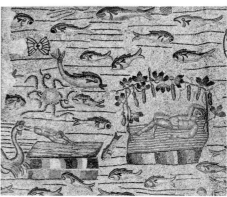

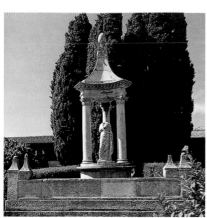

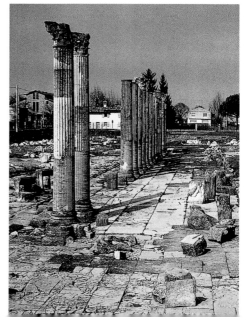

▶ Many ruins are still visible in Aquileia. Among these are the forum and portico that date back to the second century A.D.; the banks of the river port; a number of houses; and the cemetery. There are burial vaults dating between the first and the fourth century A.D.

The Sacred and Profane on Sarcophagi

Sculpture from this period is best represented by an enormous quantity of marble sarcophagi. They form a vast repertory of compositional schemes used and transmitted from one workshop to another over a long period. Those produced in Rome are not generally decorated on the back side due to the Italian custom of placing sarcophagi against the walls of a burial vault, while the Eastern variety, which were placed in the center of a sepulcher, were decorated on the front, back, and the short ends. These were often decorated as a bed on top and sometimes featured a statue of the deceased on the cover. Two sculptural masterpieces of the era are the sarcophagus of Junius Basso, where Christian themes are inserted in a classical scheme similar to a variety of sarcophagi from Asia Minor, and another of Saint Helena made of red porphyry. Porphyry usually had to be entrusted to workers who were experts in the difficult work of sculpting this material. A single scene in highest relief portrays Roman knights either giving chase to barbarians or escorting them as prisoners.

▶ A marble slab fragment depicting the multiplication of the loaves and fishes from the end of the third or the beginning of the fourth century A.D. The fragment has traces of coloring on it and was probably the front piece of a large sarcophagus. It went together with other scenes inspired by the New Testament. Rome, Palazzo Massimo alle Terme.

▶ The sarcophagus of Marcus Claudianus, circa A.D. 330–335. There are scenes of the Old and New Testaments on this complex relief. Rome, Palazzo Massimo alle Terme.

▼ A sarcophagus with the myth of Prometheus from the fourth century A.D. At the center of the relief the hero observes the body of clay that he molded and to which he will give life. Naples, Museo Archeologico Nazionale.

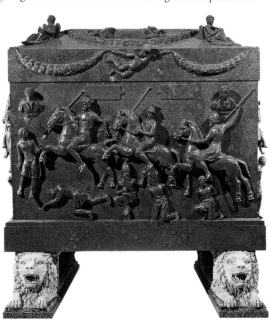

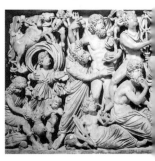

◀ The sarcophagus of Saint Helena, circa A.D. 320, restored in the eighteenth century. It perhaps was prepared for Constantine, but was then used for his mother. Vatican City, The Vatican Museums.

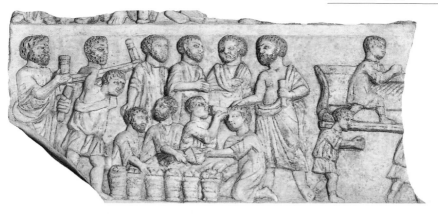

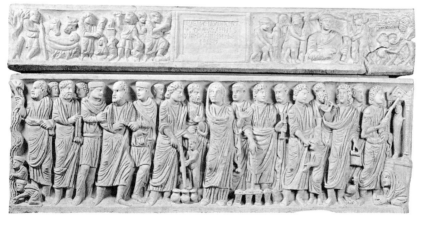

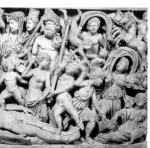

▶ The sarcophagus of Junius Basso. Scenes from the Old and New Testaments were sculpted for Junius Basso, who died in A.D. 359. Vatican City, Grotte Vaticane.

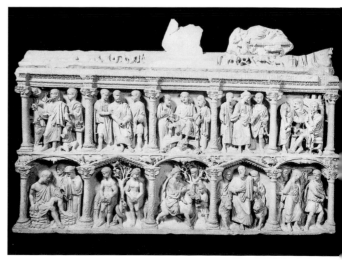

Diptychs

Derived from the tablets that imperial decrees were written on, consular diptychs made of ivory became widespread in the fourth century A.D. In the fragmentary diptych of the Lampadii family from the first half of the fifth century A.D. in Rome, a magistrate who was a fan of the games watches a chariot race in the circus.

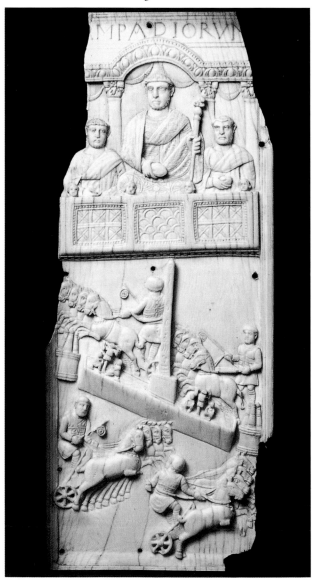

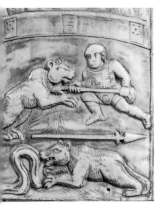

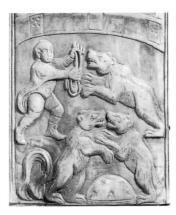

◀ A consular diptych made of ivory depicting a combat scene in an arena. Ivory diptychs were gifts for high officials who had just achieved a new position. In order to curb the exaggerated use of such extremely prestigious objects, a special law was passed in A.D. 384 establishing that they could only be presented to consuls. Paris, Louvre.

▶ The Stilicho Dyptych, circa A.D. 400. An armed Stilicho appears dressed as a consul with his wife, Serena, and his son Eucherius. Production of secular diptychs stopped in A.D. 541 when the position of consul was abolished. Ecclesial diptychs would continue to be made through the seventh century A.D. Monza, Tesoro della Cattedrale.

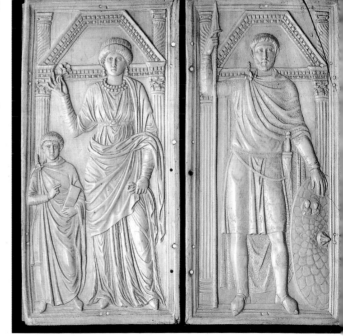

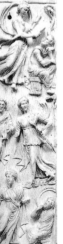

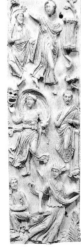

◀ An ivory diptych from the fifth century A.D. Besides being a precise expression and a record of official art from the time, these tablets cut from ivory are particu-larly interesting because they can be dated from those public offices held by the characters they portray and often contain rich symbolism. Paris, Louvre.

Theodosius and the Suppression of Pagan Worship

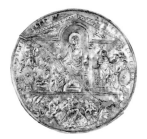

▲ *Missiorum of Theodosius,* A.D. 387–388. This large silver plate portrays Theodosius, Valentinian the 2nd, and Arcadius. It was probably a gift from the emperor—who was originally from Spain—to another Hispanic dignitary to celebrate the tenth anniversary of his reign. Madrid, Academia de la Historia.

When Constantine died, a new wave of violence fell on the imperial court. In A.D. 351 one of his sons, Constantius the 2nd, remained the sole sovereign and reinforced the position of Christianity in the empire. Constantius would nominate his nephew Julian, who would succeed him in A.D. 361. Julian's brief reign featured the final attempt to oppose the classical culture of Christianity. The young man had grown up in the cruel and treacherous climate of the imperial court, and because of this he despised Christian environments and studying ancient philosophy. He felt more akin to classical pagan traditions. Any attempt to restore pagan ritual eventually failed, however, when Julian died in A.D. 363. Power passed into the hands of a series of emperors who were often too young and worried about checking the growing barbarian horde that threatened the borders of the empire. In A.D. 379 Theodosius became ruler of the eastern empire. Thanks to a politics of compromise with the barbarians and a weak emperor in the west, he was able to keep the entire Roman empire under control. Theodosius accented the religious nature of the empire, and with two edicts in A.D. 380 and 391 he declared Catholicism the official state religion, thereby outlawing pagan rituals.

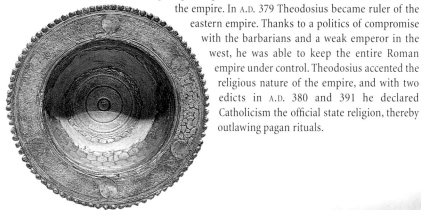

▲ A silver cup with engraved decorations from the end of the fourth century A.D. The engravings were filled with a tin alloy, silver, and black sulfur. Aquileia, Museo Archeologico Nazionale.

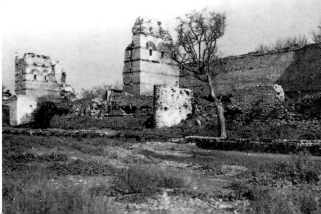

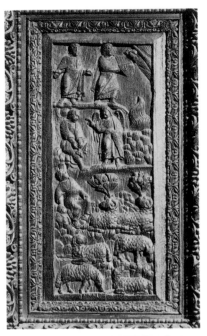

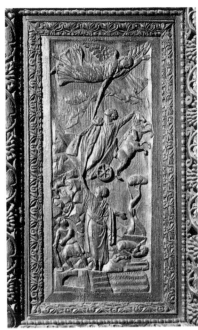

▲ These wooden panels are from the door of the Basilica of Saint Sabina, built around A.D. 420 by a rich Illyrian priest named Peter. They are among the most noteworthy works of art from Christian Rome.

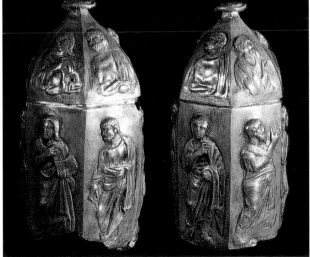

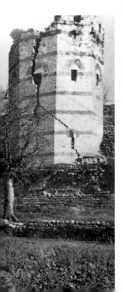

◄ A stretch of the wall built in Constantinople by Theodosius the 2nd beginning in A.D. 413, the last example of defensive architecture for the empire.

▲ These hexagonal silver relic containers from Pola, Croatia, date to the beginning of the fifth century A.D. The relic carriers portray the figure of Christ and the saints. The works were probably buried in the foundation of a church. Vienna, Kunsthistorisches Museum.

The Fall of the Western Empire

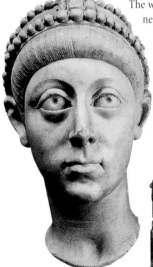

▼ Arcadius, circa A.D. 387–390. This oldest son of Theodosius ruled in the east from A.D. 383 to 408, although he left the actual governing to his ministers, Rufinus and Eutropius. Istanbul, Archeology Museum.

In A.D. 410, eight centuries after the Gauls of Brenno sacked Rome, the Visigoth troops of Alaric invaded Italy and sacked the city. They then stationed themselves in southern Gaul and founded the first barbaric kingdom that was recognized by the western court. The last positive result of the collaboration between the eastern and western empires was drafting the Theodosian Code, which Theodosius the 2nd, emperor of the eastern empire, had drawn up in agreement with Valentinian the 3rd in order to give some sort of order to the volume of legislation that had passed during the century before.

The western empire continued to be progressively dismembered by new barbaric kingdoms that formed. These were only weakly contested by emperors who governed in the shadow of powerful generals of barbaric descent. This lasted until A.D. 476 when the German leader Odoacer overthrew Romulus Augustulus, the last puppet emperor, and sent the imperial insignia to Constantinople, signaling the end of the western empire. While this year would have great significance for posterity, it did not mean much to the people of the time, who had already been experiencing the disintegration of the empire for decades.

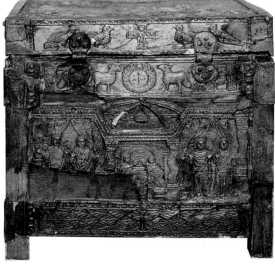

► An ivory box from the first half of the fifth century A.D. from Samaghèr. It was retrieved in fragments among the ruins of a church in Pola, Croatia, and is made of a sculpted ivory veneer reinforced by silver hardware. Venice, Museo Archeologico Nazionale.

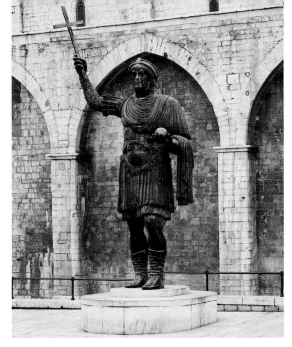

◀ This colossal statue from Barletta, more than five meters high, could be the portrait of Emperor Marcianus (A.D. 450–457). Venetians removed it from an eastern city in the twelfth century, but it was abandoned in fragments after a shipwreck.

▼ A woman's portrait, circa A.D. 400. This sculpture could be Eudocia, daughter of Bautus, the leader of the Franks. She became the wife of Emperor Acadius in A.D. 395 and died in A.D. 404. Rome, Museo Torlonia.

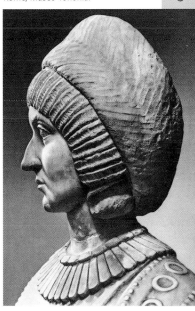

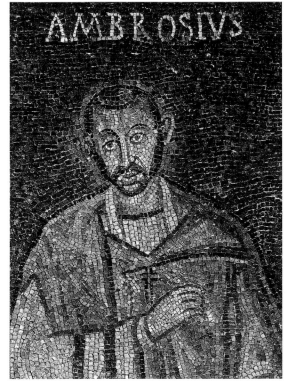

◀ Saint Ambrose, circa A.D. 400. This bishop of Milan from A.D. 374–397 held strong political influence with the emperors. In A.D. 390 he excommunicated Theodosius, who in turn made public amends. Religious authority had swayed politics. Milan, San Vittore.

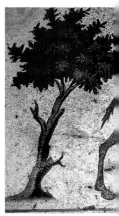

Constantinople and the Triumph of Christian Art

Because of the definitive break between Constantine and Rome's population, a new capital was founded on Bosporus between A.D. 328 and 330 in a strategic position that controlled the strait between the Marmara and the Black Sea. Constantine wanted to create a "new Rome," just as the Augustan city had been, complete with regions, a forum, a capitol, and a senate. The construction of churches dedicated to the apostles; peace (Saint Irene); and, with Constantius the 2nd, wisdom (Saint Sophia) all contributed to giving the city Christian characteristics. In these church dedications a sort of mix between pagan and Christian elements can be noted, such as the personification of abstract concepts such as peace to holy figures. This had been customary for pagan religions during the imperial period. The new capital developed quite rapidly, and already by the beginning of the fifth century A.D. there were eleven imperial palaces, fourteen churches, five markets, eight public baths, and imposing walls to defend the city from a land attack. For a thousand years, these walls would be a gigantic defensive bulwark for the city until it was stormed by the Turks in 1453.

◄ The interior of Saint Sophia in Istanbul. A large quantity of precious materials was used for decorating the church's interior, and at its inauguration in A.D. 537, the sheer brilliance of the church left believers astonished.

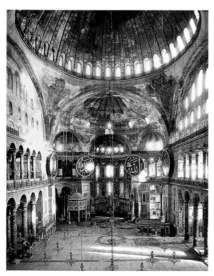

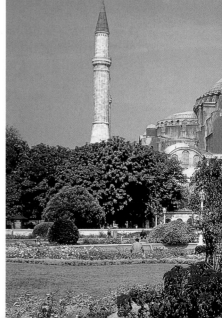

124

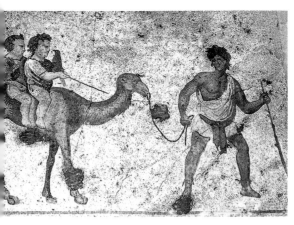

◄ A mosaic of two children on a camel's back from the fifth or sixth century A.D. While the camel was once mostly used for plowing, it soon became a traveling animal for nomads beginning about A.D. 400. The ability of these peoples to move so quickly led to notable problems in defending agricultural and coastal areas of Roman Africa from them. Istanbul, Gran Palazzo degl'Imperatori.

► A sarcophagus from Salonae, circa A.D. 320. Portraits of the deceased flank the Good Shepherd in the central arch. These are surrounded by a multitude of small figures of clients or benefactors. The piece does away with hierarchical proportions, making it already more similar to medieval iconography. Split, Museo Archeologico.

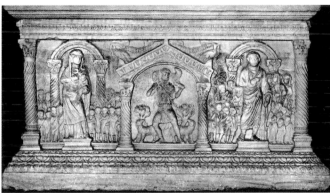

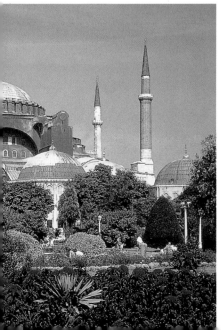

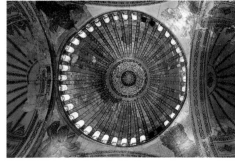

◄ Saint Sophia in Istanbul. The church represented the spiritual center of eastern Christianity, just as Saint Peter in the Vatican was the fulcrum for western Christianity.

▲ The central dome of Saint Sophia has a diameter of more than thirty meters and includes forty-four windows. The windows allow a great deal of light to enter.

Justinian and the Byzantine Empire

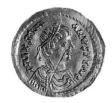

While the western empire was disintegrating, imperial troops in the east resisted the pressure of the barbarians and a central power was reinforced. The new empire was founded upon the absolute power of the emperor. This provided bureaucratic efficiency, a productive commercial base, a defensive system with a strong military, and refined diplomacy. The church assumed some roles in managing the state. A definitive consolidation of the empire was in A.D. 527, when Justinian conceived the idea to restore imperial domination over the Mediterranean basin while renewing and reconnecting with Roman traditions. He put a plan into action to re-conquer the territories of Italy, North Africa, and Spain and dedicated himself to intensive lawmaking, instituting a collection of laws that connected with the foundations of Roman law (*Corpus iuris civilis*) while at the same time integrating and adapting to any new necessities. Unfortunately Justinian's plans had too high a cost for state coffers, and military conquest proved ephemeral. At his death in A.D. 565 the empire was in a serious economic, social, and military crisis.

▲ An Ostragoth coin with a profile of Justinian from A.D. 541 to 549. The mints that were active under the Goths and then under Theoderic and his successors were Rome, Milan, and Ravenna. They continued to produce money and coins in the name of the eastern emperors. Despite hostilities between the Goths and the Byzantine Empire this money, which even portrayed the bust of the emperor, reaffirmed the imperial appearance of mints that were controlled by the Goths. Brescia, Musei Civici.

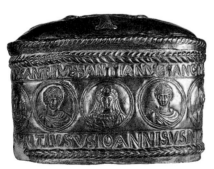

▲ A silver relic holder from the first half of the fifth century A.D. The busts of Saints Canzius, Canzianus, and Canzianilla, martyrs of the Aquileia church, are portrayed on the oval box in round frames. Grado, Tesoro della Basilica di Sant'Eufemia.

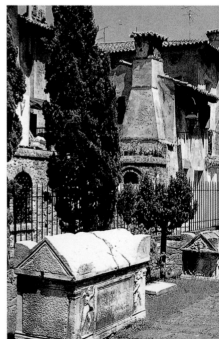

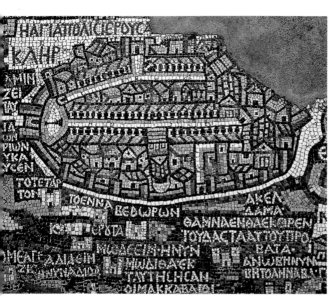

◀ A mosaic floor from fourth-century Madaba in Jordan. A map of the Middle East takes up the entire floor; this detail features a map of Jerusalem and principal landmarks of the time.

▼ The Baptistry of Sant'Elia in Grado. Bishop Nicetus (A.D. 454–455) took up the building of the first baptistry, which was later finished by Patriarch Elia (A.D. 571–586). Grado had been the commercial stop on the route to Aquileia for a long time, but after Attila fell on the region in A.D. 452 the city reaffirmed itself as an independent city. It proved to be a refuge for exiles from Aquileia and assumed an important role in the region.

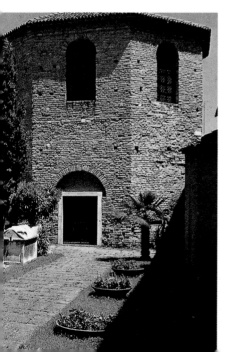

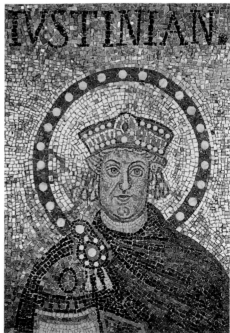

▲ An aged Justinian from the sixth century A.D. The emperor passed severe laws against pagans, Jews, and heretics but reconciled different church factions. Ravenna, Sant'Apollinare Nuovo.

Ravenna

► The Empress Theodora and her entourage, from the middle of the sixth century A.D. Theodora was an ex-actress who was fascinating and gifted with a great intelligence. For twenty-five years she was wife, adviser, and often inspiration to Justinian. She died in A.D. 548. Ravenna, presbytery of San Vitale.

Until the Augustan period, Ravenna had been an important base for the imperial fleet on the Adriatic Sea. It later developed rapidly after Honorius chose it for his imperial residence in A.D. 402. Barbarian invasions had weakened Milan's position. Situated on the Po delta and surrounded by waterways and marshes, Ravenna gave more of a guarantee in terms of defense, and being near the fortified port of Classis allowed for a quick sea escape. For these same reasons, the city was also chosen by the Ostragoth king Theodoric, who arrived in Italy at the end of the fifth century A.D. not as an invader, but as a member of the imperial federation and sent by the Byzantine emperor. Theodoric built an imperial palace whose only remnants are mosaics in Sant'Apollinare Nuovo, the church that was annexed by the palace, and a mausoleum, the monument that best sums up the era of Ostragoth culture in Italy. The mausoleum is a ten-sided building and is a throwback to the great sepulchers of the Roman emperors, yet the choice of roofing immediately identifies it with barbaric sepulchers. During the Byzantine period Ravenna became a rich and powerful city with close ties to the eastern empire. Churches that had been built at the end of the fifth century A.D. were restored and modified, and the Basilica di San Vitale was constructed.

◄ The Basilica of San Vitale in Ravenna was built between A.D. 526–548. It is a perfect example of paleo-Christian art and would be a model for the chapels of the High Middle Ages. Today it is still splendidly preserved with brilliant mosaics inside, each arranged within the building's octagonal shape.

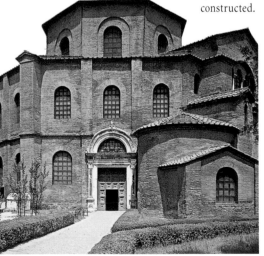

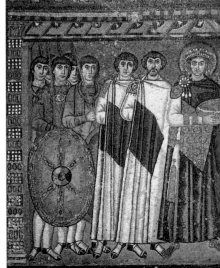

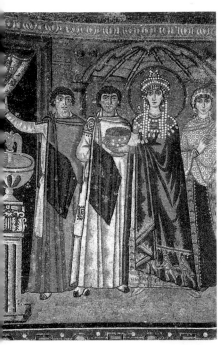

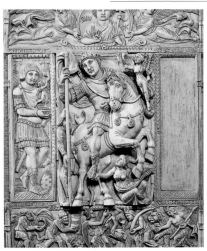

▲ The Barberini diptych, circa A.D. 550. Justinian is between pagan and Christian symbols, the personification of imperial authority. Paris, Louvre.

▼ The dome from the Arian Baptistry in Ravenna, from the beginning of the sixth century A.D. The mosaic shows a procession of the apostles and Christ being baptized.

▼ Emperor Justinian and his entourage, from the middle of the sixth century A.D. The mosaic is symmetrical with that portraying the empress and her ladies-in-waiting. Ravenna, presbytery of San Vitale.

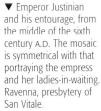

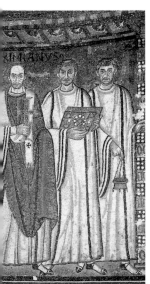

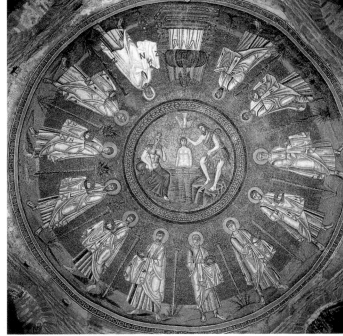

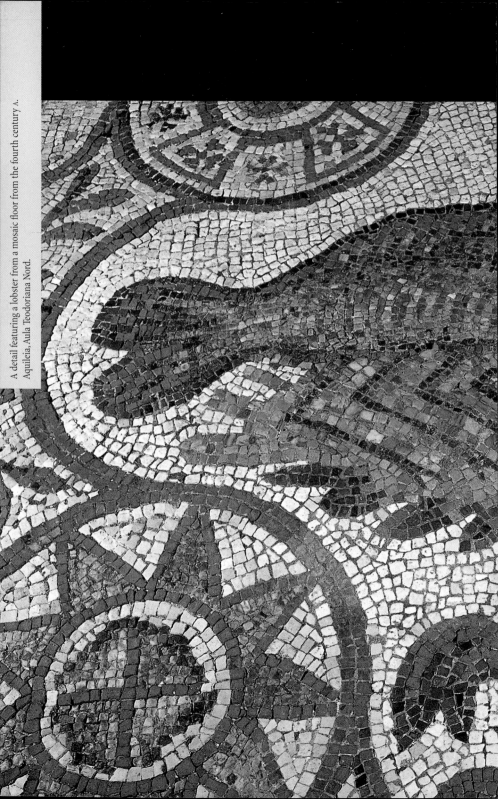

A detail featuring a lobster from a mosaic floor from the fourth century A. Aquileia, Aula Teodoriana Nord.

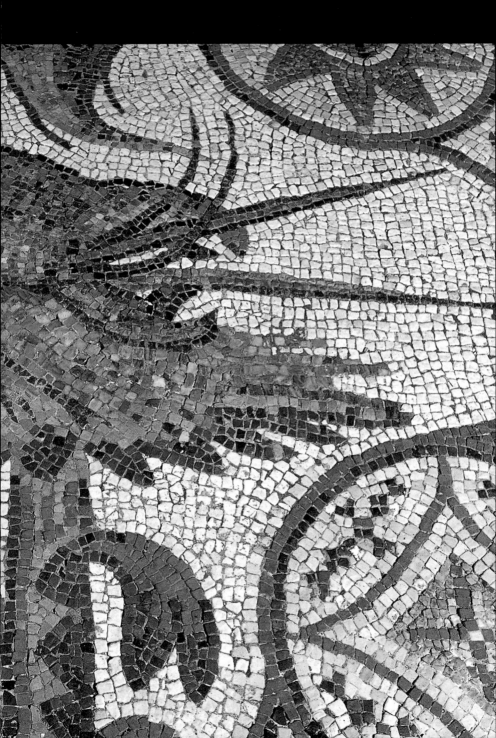

Appendixes

The Roman Empire under
Trajan (A.D. 98–117)

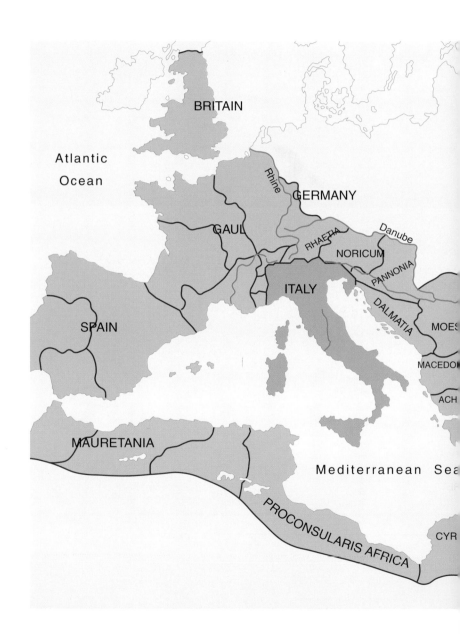

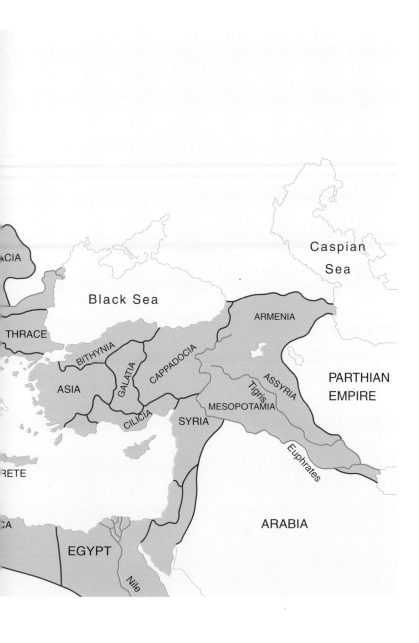

Fourth-Century Rome

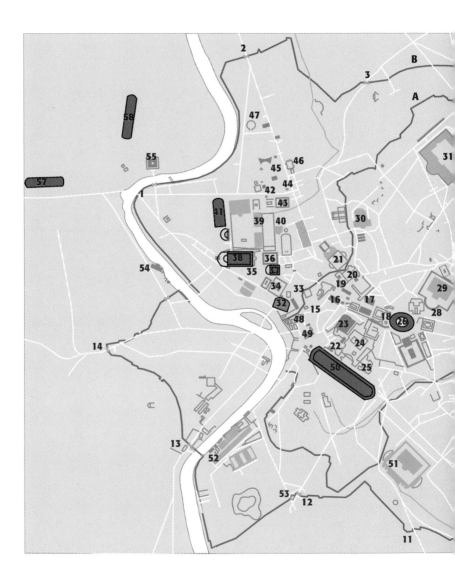

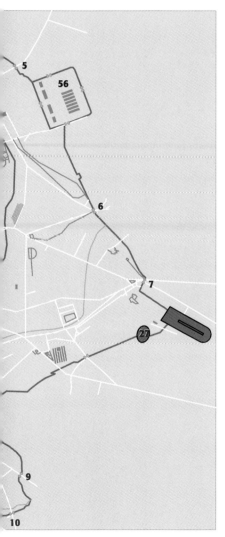

A. Severan Walls
B. Aurelian Walls
1. Triumphal Gate
2. Flaminia Gate
3. Pinciana Gate
4. Salaria Gate
5. Nomentana Gate
6. Tirburtina Gate
7. Praenestina Gate
8. Metronia Gate
9. Latina Gate
10. Appia Gate
11. Adreatina Gate
12. Ostiensis Gate
13. Portuensis Gate
14. Aurelia Gate
15. Capitol
16. Roman Forum
17. Basilica of
   Maxentius
18. Temple of Venus
   and Roma
19. Forum of Caesar
20. Forum of Augustus
21. Trajan Forum
22. House of Augustus
   and Temple of
   Apollo
23. Domus Tiberiana
24. Domus Flavia
   and Domus
   Augustana
25. Domus Severiana
26. Colosseum
27. Castrense
   Amphitheater
28. Domus Aurea
29. Baths of Trajan
30. Baths of
   Constantine
31. Baths of Diocletian
32. Theater of Marcellus

33. Temples of Apollo
   and Bellona
34. Portico of Octavian
35. Porticus Minucia
   Vetus (off Via
   Argentina)
36. Porticus Minucia
   Frumentaria
37. Theater and Crypt
   of Balbus
38. Theater and
   Porticoes of
   Pompey
39. Pantheon
40. Iseum and
   Sarapeum
41. Stadium of
   Domitian
42. Temple of Matidia
43. Temple of Hadrian
44. Antonine Column
45. Column of
   Antoninus Pius
46. *Ara Pacis*
47. Mausoleum of
   Augustus
48. Holy Site of
   Sant'Omobono
49. Boarius Forum
   (The Cattle
   Market)
50. Circus Maximus
51. Baths of Caracalla
52. Emporium
53. Pyramid of Gaius
   Cestius
54. Farnesi House
55. Mausoleum of
   Hadrian
56. Castra Praetoria
57. Circus of Caligula
58. Vatican Naumachia

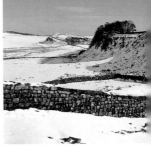

Legend

Ancient places that made up the territory of the Roman Empire are included here.

Adamklissi, a locality of Dobrudja circa sixty kilometers southwest of Constanta, Romania, where ruins of a triumphal monument of Hadrian can be found, p. 48.

Alexandria, an Egyptian city on the Mediterranean Sea founded by Alexander the Great in 332 B.C., pp. 12, 20, 36.

Amiternum, a Roman city in Sabini, present-day San Vittorino near Aquila in Abruzzo, p. 15.

Ancona, p. 47.

Antinoöpolis, a city of ancient Egypt on the left bank of the Nile founded by Hadrian in A.D. 130–131 in honor of Antinous, p. 54.

Aquileia, a Latin colony beginning in 181 B.C., which in the late imperial period hosted the imperial residence and a diocese, pp. 92, 114–115, 120, 126–127, 130.

Arles, a city of southern France and a Roman colony beginning in 46 B.C., p. 43.

Asido, a Roman city on the Iberian peninsula, present-day Medina Sidon, p. 27.

Athens, pp. 52, 54, 60.

Baia, a natural port situated on the Campanian coast between Naples and Cumae, p. 39.

Barletta, the ancient port of Canusium in Puglia, p. 123.

Benevento, a city in Campania named by the Romans after their victory against Pirro in 275 B.C., p. 45.

Bithynia, a region of Asia Minor toward the Black Sea, an independent kingdom until the death of Nicomedes the 4th in 74 B.C., then a Roman colony, pp. 52, 92.

Boscoreale, a small Vesuvian town buried by the eruption of A.D. 79, pp. 21, 36.

Britain, the name given by the Romans to the British Isles, which were occupied by Caesar in 55–54 B.C. and only completely conquered by Claudius in A.D. 43, pp. 57, 132.

Byzancena, an ancient region of Africa between the present-day Gulf of Hammamet and Lesser Syrtis, p. 108.

Byzantium, a city on the Bosporos that is present-day Istanbul, it became the capital of the empire with the name Constantinople in A.D. 330. See Constantinople.

Caorle, p. 114

Campania, p. 34.

Capua (Santa Maria Capua Vetere), one of the oldest cities of Campania, a Roman colony since 59 B.C., p. 20.

Carpentras, the ancient Carbantorate, a southern French city, p. 24.

▲ The ruins of a theater in Verulamium (St. Albans), Great Britain

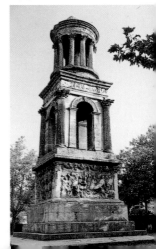

► Mausoleum of the Julii family in Glanum (Saint Rémy)

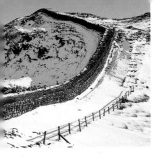

◀ A section of Hadrian's ramparts in Scotland

▶ A theater from the Augustan period in Lepcis Magna

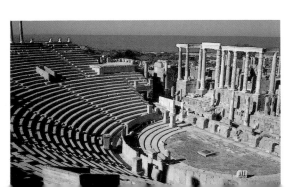

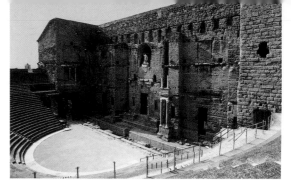

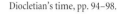
▶ A theater in Orange from the middle of the first century A.D.

Luni, the Etruscan city of Liguria, a Roman colony beginning in 177 B.C. near present-day Sarzana, p. 49.

Lusitania, a region of western Hispania corresponding to modern-day Portugal, p. 50.

Macedonia, Balkan region and homeland to Alexander the Great, it became a Roman province in 146 B.C., pp. 8, 64.

Madaba, Jordan, p. 127.

Magna Graecia, a group of Greek colonies in southern Italy and Sicily, p. 6.

Maritimae Alpes, a province instituted by Augustus in 14 B.C. in the area north of Nice on the two banks of the Var river, p. 24.

Mauretania, an ancient North African kingdom in what is today Morocco and Algeria, it became a province under Claudius, pp. 79, 108.

Medina Sidon, see Asido.

Mesopotamia, a central region of the Middle East between the Tigris and Euphrates rivers, pp. 59, 91.

Milan, once ancient Mediolanum, it became part of the Roman Empire in 194 B.C. and later the capital of the western empire, pp. 74, 102, 123, 126, 128.

Misenum, northern headland of the Gulf of Naples, it was the main naval base for Rome up until the beginning of the fifth century A.D., p. 42.

Moesia, a Roman province south of the lower Danube toward the Black Sea, this territory today is divided between Romania and Bulgaria, p. 78.

Nemausus, present-day Nîmes, one of the main cities of Narbonesis, Gaul, p. 24.

Nicea, modern-day Iznik, a city of Bithynia, which in A.D. 325 was the site of the first great ecumenical council convened to condemn the heresy of Bishop Arianus (Arianism), p. 102.

Nicomedia, today the Turkish city of Izmit, it was the ancient capital of Bithynia and was linked to Rome in the time of Nicomedes the 3rd (127–94 B.C.) and became capital of the eastern empire in

Diocletian's time, pp. 94–98.

Nîmes, see Nemausus.

Numidia, an ancient region of North Africa (Algeria) inhabited by Berber nomads, it was annexed by Rome in 46 B.C. and became a province in A.D. 38, pp. 79, 108.

Orange, the ancient Arausio, a city of Gaul colonized by Julius Caesar, where the Romans suffered a heavy defeat at the hands of the Cymbrians nearby in 105 B.C., pp. 22–23, 38.

Ostia, the ancient commercial port of Rome around which a blossoming city developed up until the fourth century A.D., pp. 46–64, 87, 93.

Palmyra, a caravan stop on an oasis between Syria and Babylon, by the first century B.C. the city had monopolized trade between the two regions; it was an independent kingdom for a brief period in the second half of the third century under Odenatus and Zenobius, pp. 58–59.

Pannonia, a Roman province between the Danube and Sava, its economy developed largely after Dacia was conquered in A.D. 106; after A.D. 380 it was invaded by the Goths and Huns, p. 78.

Pergamum, a Greek city of

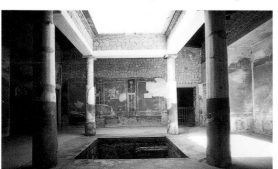
◀ The atrium of the Vettii family house in Pompeii dates to the middle of the first century A.D.

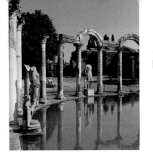

Asia Minor and capital of the Hellenistic kingdom of the Attalids, it was the center of an eclectic school for sculpture whose influence lasted through the entire Roman period, pp. 9, 20, 53.

Piazza Armerina, a city in Sicily (Enna) where an extravagant Roman villa from the beginning of the fourth century A.D. was discovered with notable floor mosaics, p. 110.

Pola, a city located on the Istrian peninsula in present-day Croatia destroyed by civil war and by Augustus, it was a blossoming city that still contains impressive ruins, pp. 40, 43, 121–122.

Pompeii, the main Campanian city destroyed by the eruption of Vesuvius in A.D. 79, pp. 32–35, 40–41, 75.

Ravenna, a city of Romagna on the Adriatic coast, it hosted the western emperor from A.D. 404 as well as the Gothic kings who followed, pp. 126–129.

Rieti, ancient Reate in Sabini, where Emperor Vespasian was born, p. 30.

Sabini, a region northeast of Rome whose citizens received their full rights as Roman citizens in 268 B.C., p. 30.

Saint-Rémy-de-Provence, see Glanum.
Salonae, modern-day Solin, an

▶ A Roman road in
Timgad (Thamugadi)

ancient Roman city six kilometers northeast of Split, Croatia, p. 99.

Santa Maria Capua Vetere, see Capua.

Saragozza Roman colony under Augustus and an important Spanish city, p. 17.

Split, a city on the Dalmatian coast that was centered around a great palace that was built by Diocletian, p. 99.

Stabiae, a city on the Gulf of Naples that was destroyed by the eruption of Vesuvius in A.D. 79, p. 35.

Syria, a kingdom on the Mediterranean coast between Egypt and Asia Minor, it was conquered by Pompey in 64 B.C. and became a province the next year, pp. 20, 56, 59.

Tarquinia, an ancient Etruscan city in Lazio, pp. 6, 25.
Tarragona, once the ancient

Tarraco on the northeast coast of Spain, it was the oldest stronghold and largest mint in the country, pp. 51, 67.

Timgad, once the ancient Thamugadi in Numidia, the city was founded by Trajan in A.D. 100 as a residence for the third legion, p. 82.

Tivoli, pp. 52, 56.

Torcello, p. 114.

Tortona, once the ancient Dertona, a city of Liguria that was once an important stop for the commerce and viability of northwest Italy, p. 32.

Treveri, once the ancient Augusta Treverorum, a city on Mosella that became a capital of the empire, pp. 106–107.

Tripolitania, a part of the Roman provinces of Africa in modern-day Libya, p. 82.

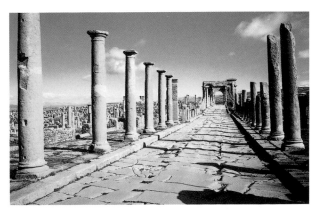

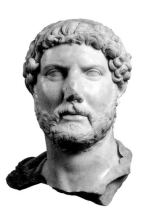

▶ Hadrian, circa A.D. 117. Rome, Palazzo Massimo alle Terme

Legend

The names of emperors, their families, and other political figures that have been cited in this book are included here.

Aemilius Paulus, a Roman consul who defeated King Perseus of Macedonia in 168 B.C. at Pidna, p. 64.

Agrippa, Marcus Vipsanius, friend and son-in-law of Augustus, he built the Pantheon and the first great public baths and died in 12 B.C., pp. 23–24, 56.

Agrippina the Younger (A.D. 15–59), the oldest daughter of Germanicus and sister of Caligula, mother of Nero and wife of his uncle Claudius, her son ordered her assassination, p. 26.

Alaric, Visigoth general who sacked Rome for three days in A.D. 410, p. 122.

Antinous, pp. 54–55, 105.

Antiochus Epiphanes the 4th, king of Syria from 175 to 163 B.C., p. 56.

Antonia, the oldest daughter of Mark Anthony and Octavia born in 39 B.C., p. 15.

Antonia Augustus (36 B.C.–A.D. 37), the youngest daughter of Mark Anthony and Octavia and mother of Germanicus and Claudius, p. 26.

Antoninus Pius (A.D. 137–161), pp. 67–69, 71.

Arcadius, eastern emperor from A.D. 383 to 408, pp. 92, 120, 122–123.

Arrius Aper, prefect of Pretorio and father-in-law to Numerian, he was executed by Diocletian in A.D. 284, p. 94.

Attalus the 1st (269–197 B.C.), king of Pergamum, p. 9.

Augustus (27 B.C.–A.D. 14), pp. 12–13, 15–18, 23–24, 26–27, 46, 50, 56.

Aurelian, born in Dacia, he became the emperor in A.D. 270; in only five years of rule he restored unity to the empire after forty years of disaster, pp. 91–93.

Balbinus, Decius Celius, senator, was emperor for only three months in A.D. 238, p. 91.

Bassianus, see Caracalla.

Bautus, leader of the Franks at the end of the fourth century, p. 123.

Caesar (100–44 B.C.), pp. 8–9, 40.

Caligula (A.D. 37–41), pp. 26–41.

Caracalla (A.D. 188–217), pp. 78–79, 81–82, 88–89, 96.

Carinus, brother of Numerian, was emperor from A.D. 283–285, p. 95.

Claudius (A.D. 41–54), the youngest son of Drusus, nephew of Tiberius, and brother of Germanicus, pp. 26, 32, 41, 57, 108.

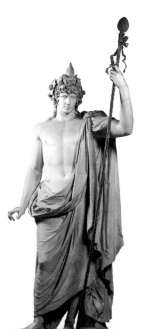

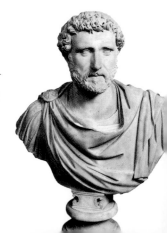

◀ Antinous dressed as Dionysos, A.D. 130–138. Vatican City, The Vatican Museums.

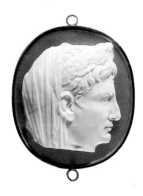

◀ Augustus , from the first decade of the first century A.D. Florence, Museo Archeologico.

Claudius the 2nd, the Goth, was of Illyrian origin and emperor from A.D. 268–270, when he died of the plague, p. 90.

Cleopatra (69–30 B.C.), this queen of Egypt had close ties to Caesar and Mark Anthony and committed suicide after being defeated at Actium.

Commodus (A.D. 180–192), pp. 64, 72–73, 78–79.

Constans the 1st, this son of Constantine was emperor in the west from A.D. 337 to 350, pp. 103, 113.

Constantina (circa A.D. 318–353), Constantine's oldest daughter, pp. 112–113.

Constantine (A.D. 306–337), pp. 71, 96, 102–104, 107, 112–116, 120, 124.

Constantius Chlorus, this general of Illyrian descent was sovereign in the west in A.D. 305–306 and died at York with his son Constantine, pp. 98, 102, 106.

Constantius Gallus, ruler of Antioch from A.D. 351 to 354, when he was executed, p. 102.

Constantius the 2nd, third son of Constantine, emperor in the east from A.D. 337 to 361, pp. 102–103, 120, 124.

Decius, originally from Pannonia, was emperor from A.D. 249 to 251, p. 93.

Diocletian, (A.D. 285–305), pp. 94–96, 98–99, 102, 114–115.

Domitian (A.D. 81–96), pp. 17, 30, 46, 60.

Drusus the Younger, p. 27.

Elagabalus (A.D. 218–222) took his name from the sun god of Emesa, p. 90.

Eucherius (A.D. 389–408), the oldest son of Stilicho and Serena, p. 119.

Eudocia, the daughter of Bautus, leader of the Franks, married Arcadius in A.D. 395 and governed in his name, p. 123.

Eutropius, an official of the court of Valens (A.D. 364–378) and author of a history of Rome from its founding to A.D. 364.

Faustina the Elder was the aunt of Marcus Aurelius and married Antoninus Pius circa A.D. 110; she died in A.D. 140 and was made a goddess, pp. 67, 69, 71.

Faustina the Younger, born near A.D. 125, daughter of Antoninus and Faustina, and wife of Marcus Aurelius, p. 71.

Gaius Caesar, the nephew of Augustus was in succession to the throne, but died in A.D. 4, pp. 25–26.

Gaius Valerius Diocles, see Diocletian.

Galerius, son-in-law and adoptive son to Diocletian, he was emperor from A.D. 305–311, p. 98.

Gallienus, (A.D. 253–268), p. 90.

Germanicus, the son of Drusus was adopted by Tiberius, but mysteriously died in A.D. 19, p. 27.

Geta, the youngest son of Septimius Severus ruled with his brother Caracalla beginning in A.D. 211, but was assassinated the year after, pp. 81–82, 88.

Hadrian (A.D. 117–138), pp. 52, 54, 55–57, 59, 60, 66, 68, 105.

Helena, the concubine of Emperor Constantius Chlorus and mother of Constantine, pp. 113, 116.

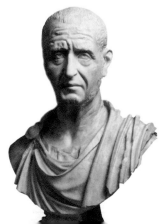

◀ Antoninus Pius. Rome, Musei Capitolini.

▶ Decius. Rome, Musei Capitolini.

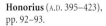
► Tiberius and Livia, A.D. 20–29. Florence, Museo Archeologico.

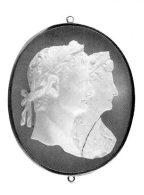

Honorius (A.D. 395–423), pp. 92–93.

Hostilian, this son of Emperor Decius became Augustus in A.D. 251 but died of the plague the same year, p. 93.

Julia, the daughter of Augustus was the wife of Marcellus, Agrippa, and finally Tiberius; after being exiled, she died in A.D. 14, p. 23.

Julia, the daughter of Titus, p. 31.

Julia Domna, the second wife of Septimius Severus possibly committed suicide at Antioch in A.D. 217, pp. 79, 83.

Julia Maesa, the sister of Julia Domna favored proclaiming Elagabalus emperor and died in A.D. 226, p. 90.

Julia Mamea, the youngest daughter of Julia Maesa and mother of Alessandro Severus, p. 90.

Julian the Apostate (A.D. 361–363), pp. 102, 120.

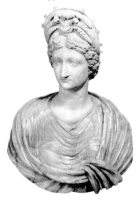
◄ Presumably a portrait of Livia from the first century A.D. Rome, Musei Capitolini.

Junius Basso, consul in A.D. 331, he built an ornate basilica of marble, pp. 108, 116–117.

Justinian (A.D. 527–565), pp. 126–129.

Lepidus, consul in 46 B.C., he concluded a pact with Mark Anthony and Octavian (the second triumvirate) and was highest pontiff until his death in 12 B.C., p. 16.

Licinius (A.D. 308–325), he was first a colleague and then an adversary of Constantine, p. 102.

Livia (circa 59 B.C.–A.D. 29), Augustus's wife, pp. 10, 16, 22, 27.

Lucius Caesar, the brother of Gaius Caesar, pp. 25–26.

Lucius Verus, the son-in-law and adoptive brother of Marcus Aurelius, with whom he ruled from A.D. 161 to 169, p. 71.

Magnetius, this usurper of the throne ruled in the west from A.D. 350 to 353, p. 103.

Marcellus, Augustus's nephew, died in 23 B.C., pp. 14, 40.

Marcianus, emperor in the east from A.D. 450 to 457, p. 123.

Marcus Aurelius (A.D. 161–180), pp. 62, 67–68, 70–71, 78–79, 92, 105.

Marcus Aurelius Antonius, see Caracalla.

Marius (156–86 B.C.), p. 8.

Mark Anthony (82–30 B.C.), was part of the second triumvirate with Lepidus and Octavian in 43 B.C.; when he was defeated at the battle of Actium in 31 B.C. he committed suicide.

Maxentius, the son of Maximian proclaimed himself emperor in A.D. 306; he was defeated by Constantine in the battle at Milvio Bridge in A.D. 312, pp. 57, 102–104.

Maximian, emperor of the west from A.D. 286–305, pp. 98, 102, 106.

Nero (A.D. 54–68), pp. 26, 28–30, 32.

Nerva, born in Narni, was emperor from A.D. 96 to 98 and was the first "adopted" emperor, p. 46.

Numerian, ruled in A.D. 284 at the death of his father Carus together with his brother Carinus, p. 95.

Octavia, Augustus's sister, wife of Marcellus and then of Mark Anthony, she was later disowned in 35 B.C., p. 15.

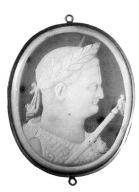

◀ Titus. Florence, Museo Archeologico.

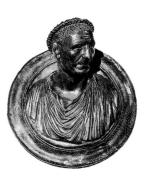

▶ Trajan. Ankara, Turkey, Museum of Archeology.

Photographic References
Electa Archive, Milan
Diego Motto, Milan
Giuseppe Schiavinotto, Rome
Luca Mozzati, Rome
The Minister of Cultural Treasures and Environment,
Office of the Archeological Superintendent of Rome

Special thanks to the museums and photographic
archives who kindly furnished the images for this book.

First published in the United States of America in 2002 by the J. Paul Getty Museum

Getty Publications
1200 Getty Center Drive
Suite 500
Los Angeles, California 90049-1682
www.getty.edu

At the J. Paul Getty Museum

Christopher Hudson, *Publisher*
Mark Greenberg, *Editor in Chief*

Project Staff

Thomas M. Hartmann, *Translator and Editor*
Hespenheide Design, *Compositor and Designer*

Library of Congress Control Number: 2001094213

ISBN: 0-89236-656-7

Printed and bound in Italy